Kabuki Plays

Kanjincho
The Zen Substitute

Adapted by
James R. Brandon
and
Tamako Niwa

A Samuel French Acting Edition

SAMUEL FRENCH

FOUNDED 1830

New York Hollywood London Toronto

SAMUELFRENCH.COM

ISBN   978-0-573-62260-1   Printed   in   U.S.A.   #13003

STORIES OF THE PLAYS

KANJINCHO is a classic of Japan's Kabuki theatre. It is the compact and tensely dramatic story of Benkei, devoted retainer of the young hero, Yoshitsune, who uses every stratagem to lead his master's party through a barrier set up by Yoshitsune's treacherous brother, who is supreme ruler of Japan. Benkei almost succeeds, but Yoshitsune is recognized. Benkei beats his master to "prove" he is not a lord. The barrier guard sees through the ruse, but is deeply impressed. He allows the group to pass. Before they go he gives Benkei a gift of rice wine. Benkei drinks prodigiously and does a brief dance in celebration of their success. This is a superbly theatrical piece, with contrasts between vigorous and stylized action and moments of delicate sadness.

THE ZEN SUBSTITUTE is a light-hearted farce of Kabuki theatre. Lord Ukyo wishes to see his girl friend on the sly, and so persuades his wife to let him perform Zen meditation under a robe in the garden. He has his servant, Tarokaja, take his place, while he slips off to his rendezvous. Lady Tamanoi discovers her husband's trick, and she in turn changes places with Tarokaja. You can imagine what happens when Lord Ukyo comes home, tipsy, and tells "Tarokaja" about his amorous adventures. The play is full of stylized comic action.

MUSIC USE NOTE

Licensees are solely responsible for obtaining formal written permission from copyright owners to use copyrighted music in the performance of this play and are strongly cautioned to do so. If no such permission is obtained by the licensee, then the licensee must use only original music that the licensee owns and controls. Licensees are solely responsible and liable for all music clearances and shall indemnify the copyright owners of the play and their licensing agent, Samuel French, Inc., against any costs, expenses, losses and liabilities arising from the use of music by licensees.

IMPORTANT BILLING AND CREDIT
REQUIREMENTS

All producers of *KABUKI PLAYS* *must* give credit to the Author of the Play in all programs distributed in connection with performances of the Play, and in all instances in which the title of the Play appears for the purposes of advertising, publicizing or otherwise exploiting the Play and/or a production. The name of the Author *must* appear on a separate line on which no other name appears, immediately following the title and *must* appear in size of type not less than fifty percent of the size of the title type.

CHARACTER DESCRIPTIONS

KANJINCHO

YOSHITSUNE—25, younger brother of the ruler of Japan, handsome, tall, noble, very refined

BENKEI—30, formerly a priest and now Yoshitsune's chief retainer, large, strong, fearless

TOGASHI—40, a noble, forthright and just, guards the barrier gate Yoshitsune needs to pass through

FIRST SOLDIER
SECOND SOLDIER } Soldiers assisting Togashi
THIRD SOLDIER

FIRST RETAINER
SECOND RETAINER
THIRD RETAINER } Retainers in Yoshitsune's party
FOURTH RETAINER

FIRST STAGE ASSISTANT
SECOND STAGE ASSISTANT } Dressed all in black they move properties on stage during performance and help the actors with their costumes, hand props, etc.

CHORUS—From six to twelve men or women. They speak or chant the passages of narration.

MUSICIANS—Optional

COSTUME DESCRIPTIONS

KANJINCHO

The basic costume for most characters in the play consists of hat, white dancing socks (*tabi*), an under *kimono*, trousers and a short robe over the *kimono*.

Yoshitsune, Benkei, and the Retainers wear costumes of identical cut: the trousers are wide and stiff and reach the ankles, the outer robe has sleeves of medium length and width and it reaches to about the hips. Benkei and

5

the Retainers wear identical small black hats (fig. A). Yoshitsune wears a straw hat (fig. G). All Retainers can have costumes of the same color. Yoshitsune's should be light, Benkei's should be darker.

Togashi wears a high, black hat that slopes backwards (fig. K). His trousers are four to six feet longer than the usual western trouser, so that they trail away behind him as he walks. The cut of these trousers is very large. His outer robe reaches the hips; the sleeves are double the length and the width of Yoshitsune's.

The Soldiers wear costumes of the same color and cut. The trousers are cut like full knickers, with leggings below the knees. They wear black socks. The outer robe is a simple vest-like garment that protrudes several inches out from the shoulders and is stiff like wings.

The Stage Assistants wear a completely black outfit: black kimono almost to the ankles, black socks, and a black hood with black net over the face. This is to make them "invisible" to the audience.

The Chorus wear costumes of one color. They wear a simple under kimono, wing-like vests of the same cut as the Soldiers, and, because they kneel through the whole performance, they can wear an apron-like piece which tucks under the knees as the lower outer garment.

If Musicians are used they are costumed as the Chorus.

CHARACTER DESCRIPTIONS

THE ZEN SUBSTITUTE

LORD UKYO—30, a noble, weak-willed and dominated by his wife, has an urge to play around

LADY TAMANOI—35, Lord Ukyo's wife, a shrew, cold, and imperious, yet with a soft woman's heart beneath the fierce exterior

TAROKAJA—25, small, wiry servant to Lord Ukyo, lives by his wits in the household

CHIEDA and SAEDA—18, maids to Lady Tamanoi, soft, feminine, and submissive

STAGE ASSISTANTS, CHORUS, and MUSICIANS (optional) as in *Kanjincho*

COSTUME DESCRIPTIONS
THE ZEN SUBSTITUTE

Lord Ukyo's costume consists of long trailing trousers, and voluminous outer robe (of the same cut as Togashi's costume). He wears no hat, so his shaven pate shows. Wears wig: bald in center, with hair drawn into top-knot in the back.

Lady Tamanoi wears simple underkimono, and a more ornate outer kimono over this. A wide sash around the waist secures the outer kimono. Wears her hair long, straight, down her back (a wig can be used). Wears white dancing socks. Chieda and Saeda are dressed in kimonos of similar cut, but made of materials with simple designs. Their hair is worn piled high on the head (wigs may be used).

Tarokaja wears a simple underkimono, wide trousers down to the ankles (of the same cut as Yoshitsune's trousers), and upper vest (of the same cut as the Soldiers in *Kanjincho*). He wears white socks and a wig like Lord Ukyo's.

Stage Assistants, Chorus, and Musicians (if used) are costumed as in *Kanjincho*.

NOTE ON MUSIC FOR
KANJINCHO and THE ZEN SUBSTITUTE

In Japan *kabuki* plays are accompanied by Musicians and Chorus who sit on stage during performance. In *Kanjincho* the Musicians play the *samisen* (a three-stringed instrument), drums, and flute. In *The Zen Substitute* there are two orchestras: one just like the one in *Kanjincho,* and one which uses only the *samisen.*

In these English language versions the stage directions describe exactly how the plays would be staged in Japan, including the placing of Musicians and Chorus on stage. The American director is free to keep this arrangement or alter it as he wishes. See page 16.

Records of authentic Japanese music, as used in *kabuki* productions in Japan, are available for both plays. The bands are cued to the sections of the play where they would normally be used.

The director has several possibilities open to him. He may use the authentic Japanese music or other music of his choice. In staging the play, he may choose to follow Japanese staging practice and place both Chorus and Musicians (who presumably would mime the playing of their instruments) on-stage. Or he may eliminate Musicians entirely, thus reducing the size of the cast, and have only the Chorus on-stage. Or he may choose to eliminate Musicians and keep the Chorus off-stage, thus reducing both the size of the cast and costuming costs.

NOTE ON THE CHORUS
in KANJINCHO and THE ZEN SUBSTITUTE

A Chorus is essential in both plays, for it is the Chorus which provides narration and commentary on the action of the play, much as does the Chorus in a Greek tragedy. The size of the Chorus, however, is something each director may decide. In Japan, the Chorus is often composed of twelve to eighteen people. An impressive effect is achieved by using, and placing on-stage, a chorus of this size. There is no reason, however, why a Chorus may not consist of half-a-dozen people, or even a single person, if this is desired.

PRONUNCIATION

The spelling of Japanese names and words used in this script approximates, as closely as possible, their sound in the Japanese language. Pronunciation is very simple, since each letter always stands for the same sound. Consonants are pronounced just as in English. The initial "g" is hard as in the English word, "gives," but a "g" in the middle of a word is nasal, as in the word "singing." Vowels are pronounced as in Italian, and as in Italian there are only five vowel sounds:

a   always as in *dot*
i   always as in *he*
u   always as in *foot*
e   always as in *bet*
o   always as in *door*

There are no dipthongs in Japanese; a vowel may be held or lengthened, but it does not change in quality to a dipthong. If two different vowels appear consecutively, they are to be pronounced as separate syllables.

You will note that the Japanese syllable is either a single vowel, or a consonant followed by a vowel. The syllable never ends with a consonant (except for the nasal sound "n"). Every syllable is stressed and is stressed equally. Thus: Yo-shi-tsu-ne; To-ga-shi Za-e-mon; Ka-ma-ku-ra.

A good system to learn the proper pronunciation of the Japanese words in the text is to first break down each word into its separate syllables. Then practice saying each syllable alone according to the above rules for pronunciation. After the sound of each syllable is clearly in mind, the word can be put together, taking care that the sound of each syllable remains the same as it was when pronounced separately. Remember: there is no *schwa* sound in Japanese, nor the "i" sound of "it," nor the "a" sound of "land."

GLOSSARY
for
KANJINCHO and THE ZEN SUBSTITUTE

agemaku—A light silk curtain at the end of the *ha-namichi*. It is raised by sticks attached to the bottom corners. A similar curtain covers the stage right entrance.

9

A-Un—Many Buddhist prayers begin with the sound "A" and end with the sound "Un," which correspond roughly to the Christian "amen" as standard phrases in the Buddhist lexicon.

Bakuya—From Chinese mythology. A sword with unmatched cutting quality.

Bodhisattva or Bosatsu—A holy man in Buddhism who has advanced to within one step of Buddhahood.

Ennen dance—Ennen means longevity. The Ennen dance, celebrating long life, was performed only by certain priests.

Five Hundred Buddhas Temple—This temple is in Kyushu, at least a week's journey from Kyoto.

Fudo—A Buddhist deity considered to have the power of suppressing evil spirits, usually represented in Japanese art as a ferocious being.

geza—A small musicians' room off stage right. The musicians can see the action of the play through wide slits in the scenery. The opening and closing music of both plays and the bells, gongs, and bass drum in *Migawarizazen* come from here.

hanamichi—A unique architectural feature of the kabuki stage. It is a raised wooden ramp which extends from stage right, through the audience to the rear of the auditorium. Its main use is to allow the actor to be close to the audience and to show himself off during long entrances and exits.

Hogan—A position and title similar to City Garrison Commander of Kyoto. Yoshitsune received this title without the permission of his brother Yoritomo, who was the supreme military ruler of Japan, and this was the cause of much of the later enmity between the two.

hyoshigi sticks—Two hard-wood sticks, clapped together to produce a ringing sound marking opening, closing, and climactic moments of the plays.

Juei era—In Japanese history the years 1182–83.

Kaga—A province in northwestern Japan, famous for its beautiful silks.

kanjincho—Literally "list of solicited subscriptions," or more simply "subscription list." Priests and monks commonly traveled about Japan soliciting contributions to build or rebuild Buddhist temples. Contributors names were entered on the *kanjincho* scroll.

kesa—A surplice, or scarf worn by Buddhist priests.

kin—One *kin* is about thirty pounds.

kiridoguchi—Literally "cut-out entrance door". It is a small hinged door, about three feet high, cut into the scenery stage left. Stage assistants use it as an entrance or exit. Actors use it only as an exit (in *Kanjincho*).

koken—An actor's personal stage assistant, dressed in the formal dress of the Tokugawa period (1615–1868). On stage he adjusts the actor's costume, hands him props, etc.

kongo staff—A special staff carried by Buddhist priests.

kotsuzumi drum—Literally "small drum." Held at the shoulder and struck with the right hand it gives a taut sound because of its small size (8 inches in diameter) and the high tension of the drum head.

kurogo—Literally "black boy." A back-stage assistant, who occasionally appears on stage, dressed completely in black, including black veil over his face. He handles the *hyoshigi* sticks, moves large stage properties, etc.

Michinoku—Old name for the northeastern part of Japan.

mie—An acting technique unique to Kabuki, in which the actor holds a pose for several seconds, tense, dynamic, at a point of great conflict in the play. It is a technique of emphasis through stopping action.

Musashi—The area around Tokyo.

nagabakama—Literally "long trousers." In Kabuki plays of Noh origin, formal court dress includes trousers that trail away some four feet behind the wearer. This style of trousers is totally unknown in the west. Trouser legs are twice as long as the wearer's legs,

11

so the wearer actually steps on the trousers as he walks.

Otafuku—One of the seven Gods and Goddesses of Good Fortune in Japan, portrayed as fat and smiling. She is the Goddess of Happiness.

nagauta music—Literally "long song," so named because its melodic structure is more extended and complicated than any other form of Japanese music. Especially developed for use in Kabuki plays.

nagauta orchestra—Usually made up of twenty to twenty-five musicians and singers. One flute (*yokobue*) player, one large-drum (*tsuzumi*) player, two to four small-drum (*kotsuzumi*) players, and sometimes one or more stand-drum (*taiko*) players sit in the front row of the orchestra. In the back row sit eight to twelve singers, who chant and sing the chorus parts of the play, and an equal number of *samisen* players (see *samisen* note).

nirvana—The ultimate desired state of being in Buddhism, variously described as the absence of all desire, the state of nothingness, the deliverance of the soul from the continuing cycle of transmigration, etc.

Noh—A ritualized form of dance-play imbued with Buddhist philosophy, which developed in 15th century Japan under the patronage of the warrior class. Masks, symbolic dance movements, musical accompaniment, and short unified play structure are typical of Noh. *Kanjincho,* based on the Noh play *Ataka,* was the first Kabuki adaptation from Noh drama (1840). *Migawarizazen,* taken from the comic play *Hanago* in 1883, was one of the last successful adaptations.

oi box—Ordinarily prayer scrolls and other Buddhist paraphernalia are carried in an *oi* box but, in *Kanjincho* the box holds Yoshitsune's armor.

oniazami thistle—A thistle noted for its hardiness.

flying roppo—*Roppo* means "six directions" and a flying *roppo* is an exit down the *hanamichi* that is, as the name implies, extremely vigorous and masculine.

Rushana Buddha—This is the Great Buddha of Nara, which still exists today. Fifty-three feet high and cast in bronze, when it was completed in 749, it was gilded with solid gold and housed in an enormous hall 284 feet long and 166 feet wide. The hall burned in 1180 and the statue was badly damaged. It is to the restoration of this hall and statue that Benkei refers.

sake—Clear rice wine.

samisen—The most important instrument in Kabuki music. It is three-stringed and usually strummed with a plectrum. It produces a very sharp, astringent sound which can be shaded to suggest a variety of emotional colorations.

samurai—A warrior. As the *samurai* class ruled Japan generation after generation, it developed into a spartan (or supposedly spartan) aristocracy. A strict ethical code—based on absolute loyalty to one's lord, dignity, and courage—regulated relations between *samurai*. Since both Benkei and Togashi act correctly under the *samurai* code, the conflict in *Kanjincho* is especially dramatic. Lord Ukyo in *Migawarizazen* shows the luxury loving, unheroic side of the system in comic terms.

Santo—The place where Benkei trained as a priest, near Kyoto.

shakujo staff—A traveling priest's staff, with large brass rings hung at the top that jingle and ring as the staff is struck on the ground.

Shingon sect—A main Buddhist sect in Japan, founded by the priest Kobo Daishi, one of the country's outstanding figures, in the 9th century.

Shinto—The religious system of revering one's ancestors and worshiping local Gods, native to Japan. Buddhism, on the other hand, came to Japan from India via China.

Shofubiku—Another name for Buddha.

Sho Hachiman—The Shinto God of War. Yoshitsune's

clan, the Minamoto, also considered Him their clan God as well.

Shungen sect—A religious order of priests, called *yamabushi*, who believed in both Buddhism and Shintoism. They practised various religious virtues deep in the mountains and often under dangerous conditions.

suzukake—The vest-like garment that is decorated with two large balls on each side of the chest.

taiko drum—A shallow drum about fourteen inches in diameter which rests on a low stand before the player. It is struck with heavy wooden sticks, usually in a slow tempo.

Todaiji temple—Literally "great eastern temple." This is the famous temple in Nara, in whose precincts is located the Rushana Buddha.

tokin hat—The small, pill-box like hat worn by Benkei and the four retainers.

tokiwazu orchestra—Composed of four singers and three *samisen* players. Its style is more lyric than *nagauta;* there are no drums nor flute.

tsuzumi drum—Larger than the *kotsuzumi* drum. It is held at the left hip and struck with the thimbled fingers of the right hand, making a metallic sound something like a rim tap on a snare drum.

yamabushi—See *Shungen* sect.

yokobue—A bamboo flute played sideways like a western flute.

zazen—Literally "sitting zen," meaning Zen contemplation while seated.

Zen—A sect of Buddhism which stresses intuitive understanding, reached through silent and solitary contemplation.

Zenkoji temple—A temple near Nagano in the center of Japan, perhaps ten days travel from Kyoto.

PROPERTY PLOT

KANJINCHO

Set Props:
All are placed U.L. under a purple cloth:

Cask with lid (fig. N).
Two *sake* gourds (fig. O).
Two trays with boxes (fig. P).
One tray with two bags of money (fig. Q).
The "kanjincho" or subscription-list (fig. D).

Hand Props:
Long practical sword for Togashi (fig. M).
9—Short swords, not drawn (can be made of wood, or if
    desired like fig. C or J).
2—Folding paper fans, used for dancing by Benkei and Yo-
    shitsune (fig. E and I respectively).
8—Non-folding paper fans, held by Togashi, Retainers, and
    Soldiers (fig. L). (In addition, similar fans are used by
    Chorus and Musicians).
5—Buddhist rosaries, for Benkei and Retainers (fig. B).
An *oi* box for Yoshitsune (fig. F).
A five-and-a-half foot staff for Yoshitsune (fig. H).

PROPERTY PLOT

THE ZEN SUBSTITUTE

Set Props:
All are placed U.L. under a purple cloth:
Cask with lid (same as *Kanjincho;* fig. N).
An ornate outer robe, which is used to cover Lord Ukyo
    when he meditates in the garden.

Hand Props:
5—Folding fans for Lord Ukyo, Lady Tamanoi, Tarokaja,
    Chieda and Saeda. (fig. E or I).
2—Small trays, one with a tea cup on it, one with cakes on
    it. Off-stage R. for Chieda and Saeda.
A vari-colored robe given to Lord Ukyo by his girl friend.
    Off-stage at the end of the *hanamichi* (raised ramp) for
    Lord Ukyo.

15

MUSIC FOR KABUKI PLAYS

Authentic Kabuki music, recorded in Japan specifically for use with these adaptations, is available on high fidelity long-playing records.

The bands of each recording are cued to match the music cues given in the text of the plays.

Each play has its own distinctive music, and hence its own separate recording.

The recordings are priced at $6 each. When ordering, please indicate by title the play for which the record is desired.

16

KANJINCHO

A KABUKI PLAY
By NAMIKI GOHEI

Adapted by

JAMES R. BRANDON
TAMAKO NIWA

KANJINCHO

As we enter the theater the traditional Kabuki curtain of broad green, rust, and black stripes is closed; the house lights are partially dimmed. In a few moments two sharp claps are heard from backstage, wood against wood, as the stage manager signals the start of the performance with his HYOSHIGI sticks. From off-stage right comes the cry "Hoo-yoo!", and the three musicians in the off-stage music cage (GEZA) take up the opening music of Kanjincho: first, the quavering, high pitched notes of a flute, then the measured beating of drums. (MUSIC CUE NO. 1) The sounds drift clearly through the light silk curtain. The audience settles down. Then two more claps of the stage manager's sticks signal that the cast is in place. The drumming rapidly increases in tempo and a stage assistant (KYOGEN KATA), kneeling beside the left proscenium arch, begins to beat out a furious tatoo with two wood clappers on a board in front of him. Just as the crescendo of sound reaches its peak another stage assistant, robed and hooded in black, runs swiftly across the stage pushing the curtain before him. (FADE MUSIC NO. 1)

Before us is revealed the sweeping expanse of the ninety-foot wide Kabuki stage, its full area suffused with light and reflecting warmly on the polished surface of the cypress dance floor. The setting is simple and stylized, representing as it does, the Noh stage. On a backpiece and two side pieces, is painted a background of light tan wooden planking, and a single gnarled pine tree flanked by bamboos. The series of slits in the scenery stage right show the location of the off-stage musicians' cage. Except for a small area

19

*upstage left, where a small group of hand properties
is placed, partially covered by a purple silk cloth,
the entire area of the stage is available for the action
of the play. There are three entrances. A colorfully
striped curtain (KIRIMAKU) covers the large entrance stage right. On the opposite side of the stage
is a small door (KIRIDO-GUCHI), used by the stage
assistants who are stationed on the left of the stage
and by actors for less important exits. The main
entrance, however, is the "flower way" or HA-
NAMICHI, a raised platform which leads from the
rear of the auditorium, through the audience, to the
right side of the stage, and which serves as an ex-
tension of the stage proper into the audience.*

*A "long-song," or NAGAUTA, orchestra of twenty-two men
can be seen formally seated at the rear of the stage,
singers and SAMISEN (a three stringed instrument)
players in the top row, and the musicians who play
the small hand-drums (TSUZUMI and KOTSUZUMI),
the larger stand drums (TAIKO), and the flute (YO-
KOBUE) in the bottom row. They wear identical black
kimonos and wide-shouldered outer garments of deep
blue marked with the crest of the Ichikawa family,
the famous Kabuki acting family that originally pro-
duced Kanjincho.*

*There is a moment of silence as the off-stage music stops.
(MUSIC CUE NO. 2) Then slowly the "long-song"
flutist lifts his instrument to his lips, a drummer
deliberately raises his sticks and they begin to play.
The curtain stage right flies open and Togashi,
three soldiers, and a sword bearer enter in stately
procession. They move slowly, deliberately, using
the sliding step of Noh dance. The foot never leaves
the floor. This style of movement is used by all
the characters in Kanjincho. Each controlled movement blends into the next, so that the character
appears to glide, rather than walk.*

When Togashi reaches center stage he stops, pivots slowly, and faces the audience. It is obvious that he is a SAMURAI, *for he wears the sumptuous ceremonial dress of nobility. His outer kimono is a voluminous affair of pale blue brocade figured with white and silver cranes. Its sleeves almost touch the floor. His legs are encased in the long trousers of court dress* (NAGABAKAMA), *which trail away a full four feet behind him. He carries a fan in his right hand. His face and hands are pure white except for black lip and eye markings. Togashi addresses the audience directly, in a stately, half-chanting style of speech.* (*FADE MUSIC NO. 2*)

TOGASHI. I stand before you here at the Kaga barrier gate! I, Togashi-Zaemon! Our Lord Yoritomo has commanded barriers to be raised throughout the realm to apprehend his younger brother Yoshitsune now reported fleeing northward toward Michinoku. The rift between the brothers is deep and Yoshitsune is said to have disguised himself as a priest in order to escape. We are strictly ordered by Our Lord Yoritomo to stop and investigate every passing priest. In faithful duty I guard this barrier for Our Lord! I command you all to be of this same mind. (*No flicker of expression has crossed* TOGASHI's *face, composure being one of the highest virtures of the* SAMURAI *code.*)

FIRST SOLDIER. (*Replying strongly, but also without any visible expression.*) Already the heads of three doubtful priests hang from the trees!

SECOND SOLDIER. As you command, every priest shall be brought before you!

THIRD SOLDIER. Captured! Bound on the spot!

FIRST SOLDIER. We are alert . . .

ALL THREE SOLDIERS. . . . ever on guard!

TOGASHI. Well spoken! Seize each and every priest who attempts to pass! We shall put at ease the mind of Our Lord of Kamakura.[1] Now, all of you to your posts!

[1] Yoshitsune's brother Yoritomo had several titles. He was

ALL THREE SOLDIER. As you command, sir!

(*MUSIC CUE NO. 3. There is a shrill cry from the flute,
followed by metallic beats on the* TSUZUMI *drum.*
TOGASHI *turns and slowly leads his small procession
across the stage, this movement symbolizing their
arriving at the barrier. The soldiers kneel in a row
upstage. The sword bearer kneels directly behind*
TOGASHI, *holding the sword before him in readiness.
From under the purple property cloth* TOGASHI'S
personal stage assistant [KOKEN] *brings out a black
lacquered cask ornamented with gold.* TOGASHI *seats
himself on it. Another stage assistant arranges the
folds of his costume.*)

FULL CHORUS. (*To flute and drum accompaniment the
eight singers seated at the rear of the stage tell the tale
of* YOSHITSUNE'S *wanderings.*)
Their travel garments are those of a priest . . .
Their travel garments are those of a wandering priest,
    with sleeves wet by dew and tears.
The time is the tenth night of the second moon.
    The tenth night of the second moon.
And so having left the capital on a moonlit night . . .
    CHORUS LEADER. (*The lead singer continues the story
of the past.*)
Passed is the Mountain of Osaka,
    Before whom those coming and going part,
    Where friends and strangers meet.
Beautiful the hills,
    Shrouded by the mists of spring.

(*The curtain at the rear of the* HANAMICHI *flies up and*
    YOSHITSUNE *enters. Using quick sliding steps he
    moves down the* HANAMICHI *toward the stage, then
    sees* TOGASHI *and the soldiers at the barrier. He*

---

the Shogun, or supreme military ruler of Japan. He was also
the Lord of Kamakura, for he ruled from the city of
Kamakura.

stops and turns back toward the audience. For a moment he poses, a subdued tragic figure. He wears a dark purple kimono and pale green trousers. His long hair is gathered together and falls down his back. His face, hands, and dancing socks [TABI] are pure white. As part of his disguise he carries a large coolie's hat and a pilgrim's staff. The blue OI box strapped to his back supposedly contains BENKEI's sutras and other religious objects; actually it contains YOSHITSUNE's armor. Next, YOSHITSUNE's four retainers stride purposefully down the HANAMICHI one by one. They pass their master and form a line between him and the stage. They wear priests' vestments and carry Buddhist rosaries. Each has a short sword at his waist.)

FULL CHORUS. (*Continuing the story of their journey.*)
By furtive ship,
Through distant paths of waves,
Arriving, now at last,
At Kaizu Bay.

(At this point BENKEI moves quickly down the HANAMICHI. He wears a priest's pill-box hat and vestments. He is an imposing figure dressed entirely in black brocade silk figured with gold. As YOSHITSUNE turns to him, the retainers kneel. FADE MUSIC NO. 3.)

YOSHITSUNE. So, Benkei. The roads ahead are blocked as you say. And this was our last hope. I know now I shall never see the North. For myself I have decided: rather than suffer an ignoble death at the hand of some nameless soldier I shall take my own life first. But I must consider your wishes, too, as I did in disguising myself a common porter. At this crucial moment have you any suggestions?

FIRST RETAINER. My Lord, why do we carry these swords? When shall they be painted with blood? Now is the crucial moment of My Lord's life.

SECOND RETAINER. Let us resolve! Cut the soldiers down! We shall fight our way through this barrier!

THIRD RETAINER. The years of obligation to Our Lord shall be repaid today! We must pass through, My Lord!

FIRST, SECOND, and THIRD RETAINERS. (*They rise, hands on the hilts of their swords.*) We *shall* pass through! (*They turn to go, but the* FOURTH RETAINER, *an older man, blocks their path with an imperative gesture and* BENKEI *speaks.*)

BENKEI. Stop! Wait a moment! (*Reluctantly the three retainers return to their kneeling positions.*) A crisis is no time for rash action. If we fight now, even though we succeed, the news will travel ahead making it all the more difficult to pass further barriers. (*Very respectfully to* YOSHITSUNE.) It was with this in mind that My Lord was asked to remove his priest's vestments and assume the role of a mountain porter when first My Lord put this matter in my charge. And now, My Lord, I beg you, pull your hat low over your eyes and make a pretense of being exhausted. If you will but follow behind us, far in our rear, surely no one will suspect who My Lordship is.

YOSHITSUNE. You plan well, Benkei. (*To the chaffing retainers.*) We shall do exactly as Benkei says.

THE FOUR RETAINERS. (*Bowing slightly.*) As Our Lord commands.

BENKEI. Then pass peacefully on.

THE FOUR RETAINERS. We obey.

(*MUSIC CUE NO. 4.* BENKEI *passes* YOSHITSUNE *and moves onto the stage to the accompaniment of* SAMISEN *music. The retainers follow closely behind.*)

FULL CHORUS.
And so the travelers,
    Bent upon passing through,
    Drew near the barrier gate.

(*There are irregular metallic taps from the* TSUZUMI

drum. Still on the HANAMICHI, YOSHITSUNE *ties his hat low over his eyes, then moves slowly onto the stage, taking a position between* BENKEI, *who is almost center stage, and the retainers who are kneeling in a row upstage right. His personal stage assistant places a small stool for him to sit on, and arranges his costume.* YOSHITSUNE *poses with his head low, clasping the pilgrim's staff over his shoulder. Though he remains motionless in this position throughout most of the play, his noble bearing is such that we are always aware of his presence.* FADE MUSIC NO. 4)

BENKEI. (*Faces front and speaks in a dignified manner befitting a priest.*) Ho there! We are priests who wish to pass!

TOGASHI. What's that? Priests, you say? (*In all his dignity he rises, strides forward, and addresses* BENKEI *in measured tones.*) Now my friends, know that this is a barrier!

BENKEI. (*Facing* TOGASHI, *but feigning deference.*) I know, sir. Throughout the country priests are now soliciting contributions for the rebuilding of the temple Todaiji in the Southern Capital. It is our honored mission to be dispatched to the Northern Provinces.

TOGASHI. A praiseworthy project, indeed. However, the very purpose of this barrier is to stop priests like yourselves. You shall find it very difficult to pass.

BENKEI. This is hard to understand. What can it mean?

TOGASHI. Relations between Our Lord Yoritomo and the Hogan[2] having become strained, three years ago Yoshitsune left his brother's service. Now he flees to the north, disguised as a priest, to seek the aid of his friend Hidehira. Hearing this the Lord of Kamakura has caused these barriers to be raised. (*He draws himself up and*

---

[2] Another name for Yoshitsune.

speaks deliberately.) Know you that I am in command of this barrier!

FIRST SOLDIER. We stand guard with orders to detain all priests!

SECOND SOLDIER. And now before us, behold, many priests!

THIRD SOLDIER. We shall not allow . . .

THE THREE SOLDIERS. . . . even one to pass!

BENKEI. Your orders are to stop all those *disguised* as priests, are they not? They surely say nothing of stopping real priests.

FIRST SOLDIER. (*Not sharing* TOGASHI's *lofty politeness, he speaks roughly and to the point.*) Say what you will. Yesterday we killed three priests!

SECOND SOLDIER. So your saying you are real priests will not excuse you!

THIRD SOLDIER. And if you try to pass by force . . .

FIRST, SECOND, and THIRD SOLDIER. (*In unison.*) . . . not one of you will survive!

BENKEI. (*Reacting with mock horror.*) And these priests you beheaded . . . Was one Yoshitsune?

TOGASHI Who can say? (*Speaks commandingly.*) It is useless for you argue. No priest . . .

THE THREE SOLDIERS. (*With great force.*) . . . shall pass this barrier!

(TOGASHI *imperiously turns his back on* BENKEI, *kicking the long trailing ends of his trousers as he does so. He strides back to his former position stage left and resumes his seat.*)

BENKEI. Monstrous horror! (*Turning to the retainers, but speaking loudly for* TOGASHI's *benefit.*) Why should such misfortune be ours? Human strength is powerless against such unforeseen fate! But at least we shall be killed with honor. Come, draw near. Let us perform our last rites!

THE FOUR RETAINERS. We shall, sir.

BENKEI. (*Gravely.*) This is our final rite! (*MUSIC CUE NO. 5. So saying he moves majestically up right where two stage assistants tie back the long sleeves of his kimono and hand him a scarlet Buddhist rosary. Meanwhile the retainers form a square center stage; they kneel, their hands folded in an attitude of meditation. With a quick glance at* TOGASHI *to see how he is taking all this,* BENKEI *moves swiftly into the square, and as the chorus sings, dances a prayer to the gods.*)

FULL CHORUS. (*To full orchestra accompaniment.*)
To detain here Yamabushi priests,
    Who are versed in the austere teaching of *En no Ubazoku,*
    Whose bodies and spirit are one and the same with the Lord Buddha . . .
    (BENKEI *raises his arms in supplication to the heavens.*)
Surely the Gods will look with disfavor upon this impious act,
    The wrath of God
    Yuya Gongen shall strike this spot!
    (*In simulated anger* BENKEI *leaps high in the air and stamps loudly upon the floor.*)
"On A Bi Ra Un Ken" . . .
    So chanting they rubbed the beads of their rosaries in prayer.

(BENKEI *rises to his full height and with a sweeping upward motion begins to rub the beads of his rosary. The others follow suit. The beads of the rosaries buzz and chatter. Then the retainers turn their backs to* BENKEI, *clap their hands in unison, and kneel, hands still folded in prayer. The tableau thus formed is similar to a statue grouping seen in many temples, that of Buddha, protected on the four sides by his kneeling guardian angels, thus implying their closeness to Buddha. FADE MUSIC NO. 5.*)

TOGASHI. (*Suspicious, he determines to test* BENKEI'S

story.) A noble decision, to die. However, you mentioned a mission of soliciting for the Todaiji Temple. If this is so surely you cannot be without a list of contributors. (*An order.*) Bring out this *Kanjincho!* I demand to hear it!

BENKEI. What? (*Momentarily stunned.*) You . . . you say read the *kanjincho* list?

TOGASHI. Read it I say!

BENKEI. (*His confident voice betrays nothing.*) It shall be done. (*He moves up stage right, where a stage assistant hands him a scroll.*)

CHORUS LEADER.

Ah, were there but a *kanjincho!*

(*MUSIC CUE NO. 6.*)

Instead, from the *oi* box he draws a single unused letter scroll,

And calling it the *kanjincho,*

He boldly reads aloud.

BENKEI. (*Moving back to center stage, he unrolls the scroll and, holding it so* TOGASHI *cannot see it, pretends to read the dedicatory passage. As* BENKEI *is a priest, he has a considerable knowledge of Buddhist ritual and is able to make up a plausible passage.*) Even Buddha, like the autumn moon, has taken refuge in the dark clouds of death. (TOGASHI *rises and stealthily begins edging toward* BENKEI.) Who then, in this world, should be surprised that life is but a long night's dream! (*Suddenly* BENKEI *senses* TOGASHI'S *presence, and he whirls to face him. The two pose for a moment, glaring angrily at each other. Then* TOGASHI, *his suspicions confirmed, strides back to his position stage left and regally resumes his seat. Uncertain whether he has been found out or not,* BENKEI *determines to brazen it out. With a flourish he unrolls the scroll once more and in even louder tones than before continues to "read" from the* KANJINCHO.) In the Middle Ages, there once lived an Emperor whose name was Shomu! Having lost his beloved wife, his grief became too much for him to bear. The tears flowed from his eyes in a continous chain; his cheeks were never dry.

To aid her advance as a Bodhisattva, he then built in her memory the great Rushana Buddha, the same that burned to the ground in the era of Juei. I, the priest Chogen, lamenting the loss of this place of worship, have received the Imperial Order to solicit throughout the provinces to rebuild this holy temple. I appeal to priests, high and low, and to laymen alike. He who contributes even a trifling amount shall live in ease in this world and shall sit among thousands of lotus in the next. I address you most reverently! (*FADE CUE NO. 6.*)

CHORUS LEADER. (*MUSIC CUE NO. 7.*)
He reads as if challenging the heavens to reverberate!

(BENKEI *rolls up the scroll with utter composure and is about to turn away. FADE MUSIC NO. 7.*)

TOGASHI. (*There is little doubt in* TOGASHI'S *mind that this is* YOSHITSUNE'S *party, yet he is impressed by* BENKEI'S *bold improvisation. Rising, he decides to test* BENKEI *further.*) I see. I have heard the *kanjincho* now, and should have no further doubts. Nevertheless, let me put a few questions to you. In this world Buddha has many kinds of followers. There are some who show a warlike appearance, and who, it is difficult to believe, are true disciples of the religious austerities. Is there an explanation for this?

BENKEI. (*Without hesitation he fabricates a plausible answer.*) There is indeed a simple explanation. It is the stern prescript of the Shungen Order, in which the principles of Buddha and Shinto combine, that its followers should wander through the precipitous mountains, there to undergo hardship and pain, subduing wild beasts and poisonous reptiles which are harmful to the world, and showing compassion toward their fellow men. Thus do they accumulate meritorious works as was our Lord Buddha's command. Thus do they save evil and lost souls and show them the way toward Nirvana. They pray for purity; they pray for the brightness of the sun and

moon and for the everlasting peace of the world. In this
way, within themselves they nurture the twin virtues of
stoicism and benevolence, while outwardly they conquer
evil and subdue heretical doctrines in a warlike manner.
All is Shinto and Buddha . . . the one-hundred-eight
beads of the rosary representing the multitudinous bless-
ings of the Gods!

TOGASHI. (*Pressing another question without pause.*)
You appear to be followers of Buddha, wearing a priest's
kesa vestment. Why then do you wear a pilgrim's *tokin*
hat at the same time?

BENKEI. The *tokin* hat and the *suzukake* vestments
are like the warrior's helmet and armor. With the sharp
sword of Amida Buddha at his side, and breaking a path
with the Kongo staff, the pilgrim crosses the highest
mountains and the most dangerous places.

TOGASHI. I know that priests carry the Shakujo sceptre,
with its soft sounding bells. But how does carrying a
Kongo staff protect a pilgrim's body and limbs?

BENKEI. A foolish question! The Kongo staff has been
famous as the pilgrim's staff since first used by the Holy
Arara, the divine being who lived in the Dantaloka
Mountains in India, and under whose guidance our
Buddha first accumulated meritorious deeds. It was this
seer who gave to our Buddha the new name of Shofubiku
in recognition of his pupil's great faith and strength of
purpose. The spirit of Buddha dwells within the staff!
As a child grows in his mother's womb, so the spirit of
Buddha grows within us all!

TOGASHI. How has this tradition been handed down?

BENKEI. Our predecessors carried it as the holy staff
of Our Lord Buddha when traveling in the mountains and
valleys and this has become the practice down through
the ages!

TOGASHI. Though a priest, you wear a sword. Is this
merely a symbol of defense, or is it used to do physical
harm?

BENKEI. Like the bow of the scarecrow, it serves to

frighten our enemies. At the same time we do not hesitate to strike down those evil beasts and poisonous snakes, and human beings as well, that violate Buddha's law or the Princely Way. For with one death many lives may be saved!

TOGASHI. One can, of course, cut down a solid object, that obstructs the eye, but what of those formless evils that may obstruct Buddha's law or the Princely Way? With what would you cut them down?

BENKEI. What difficulty is there in destroying formless evils? One would dispel them with the nine-word Shingon prayer!

TOGASHI. (*Moving in toward* BENKEI, *he presses another series of questions without pause.*) Now tell me, what is the significance of your dress?

BENKEI. It is patterned in the likeness of the ferocious deity Fudo!

TOGASHI. What is the meaning of your *tokin* hat?

BENKEI. It is the headdress of the five wisdoms, its twelve folds symbolizing the affinity of cause and retribution!

TOGASHI. (*Moves in another step.*) And the *kesa* vestment you wear about your neck?

BENKEI. (*He moves in toward* TOGASHI.) It is a *suzukake* of persimmon in color, signifying the nine stages of Buddha's paradise!

TOGASHI. Why the bindings about your legs?

BENKEI. They are the black leggings of the Shingon Sect!

TOGASHI. And your eight-knobbed straw sandals?

BENKEI. In the spirit of treading on the eight-petaled lotus!

TOGASHI. (*Almost spitting it out.*) And the air you breathe?

BENKEI. (*They are face to face, just a few feet apart.* BENKEI *controls himself, but he is trembling with anger. For a moment they glare at each other in tableau.*) In the

holy sutras, the beginning and the end, the two reverend
sounds—"*A* and *UN*"*!*

TOGASHI. (*Still pressing.*) And now one final question.
What is the meaning of the nine-word Shingon prayer!
(*For a moment* BENKEI *cannot reply.* TOGASHI *senses the
lapse he has been waiting for. He draws back a pace, and
raises his fan in a commanding gesture. He speaks imperiously.*) Come, come! What do you say!

BENKEI. (*The question is far beyond* BENKEI'S *knowledge of Buddhism. He is furious with* TOGASHI *and
being by nature an impetuous and proud man, he is
sorely tempted to abandon his pose.* BENKEI *is renowned
as a warrior; he knows he could easily defeat* TOGASHI.
*Nevertheless, he controls himself and launches into a
brilliant improvisation of Buddhist jargon.*) This nine-
word prayer is a precious secret of the Shingon faith and
its meaning is most difficult to explain. But to still your
doubt I shall undertake to do so. The nine words are:
Rin Byoh Toh Sha Kai Chin Retsu Zai Zen! Before you
draw your sword, first, you must strike your teeth thirty-
six times with hands folded in supplication. Then, with
the thumb of your right hand, you draw four lines from
earth to sky and five lines from horizon to horizon.
Simultaneously, you rapidly incant the blessing *"kyuu
kyuu nyo ritsu ryoo."* So doing, all evil—the evil of
worldly passions and the devil of heresy—will disappear
like frost before the vapors of steam. Sharp and shining,
the prayer cuts through to the very heart of the world's
darkness. In this it is beyond compare, even to the
miraculous sword of Bakuya, and the warrior who utters
it cannot fail to defeat his enemy! Now . . . have you
any further questions regarding our religious practices?
I shall reply to them all in full, that you may share in
the power of their virtue, which is all-embracing and
infinite! Engrave these words on your heart, but reveal
their secrets to no one! Oh, Gods and Bodhisattvas of
Japan, I call upon you to witness the words I most
reverently speak! I bow before you! (*He does, then*

turns to TOGASHI.) I speak to you with utmost respect.
FULL CHORUS. (*MUSIC CUE NO. 8. To* SAMISEN *music.*)
The barrier guard seems impressed.

(BENKEI *dances a few steps expressive of his success, then he and* TOGASHI *pose in tableau:* BENKEI *with the scroll held high as in triumph, and* TOGASHI *with his fan held over his head. This is a high point of the play. From the audience come loud cries of "Well done!", "We've waited for this!", "Like your father before you!" FADE MUSIC NO. 8.*)

TOGASHI. (TOGASHI *is certain they are* BENKEI *and* YO-SHITSUNE, *yet* BENKEI *has not faltered in his defense of his master. Impressed,* TOGASHI *decides to let them pass.*)
That I should have doubted such honorable priests even for a moment. I should like to be added to your list of contributors. Guards, bring gifts for the priests!
THE THREE SOLDIERS. Yes, sir.

(*The mood relaxes perceptibly. MUSIC CUE NO. 9. Quiet* SAMISEN *music underlies the following actions.* TOGASHI *returns to his seat stage left.* BENKEI *gives the scroll to his stage assistant up right and receives a rosary. At the same time,* THE THREE SOLDIERS *pick up gift trays which have just been brought in through the small door stage left by* TOGASHI'S *stage assistant. The soldiers place the trays center stage and return to their kneeling positions up stage of* TOGASHI.*)

FULL CHORUS.
On wide stands, brought forth by the guards,
    A ceremonial skirt of pure white silk,
    Many rolls of Kaga silk,
    A mirror and golden coins.
        (*FADE MUSIC NO. 9.*)

TOGASHI. Though the gifts are small it would be ac-
credited as a meritorious deed for me should you accept
them on behalf of the priests of Todaiji. Respectfully, I
beg you accept them.

BENKEI. (*Standing before the gifts, ready to receive
them, he speaks impressively.*) You are indeed a benevo-
lent Lord. There can be no doubt of your peaceful, happy
existence in this world and the next. (*He rubs his rosary
over the gifts in blessing.*) One thing more. We will be
traveling through the neighboring provinces, not return-
ing to the capital until the middle of the fourth moon. I
beg you to keep the larger articles for us until then. (*He
kneels before the gifts. When he rises he takes only the
two bags of money from the center tray. These he gives
to two of the retainers.*) Now, pass through!

THE FOUR RETAINERS. Yes, sir!

BENKEI. (*He takes out his fan, flips it open, and holds
it in front of him. His actions appear unconcerned, but
his voice betrays his anxiety over their delicate situation.*)
Go! Go now! Hurry!

THE FOUR RETAINERS. We go, sir!

CHORUS LEADER. (*MUSIC CUE NO. 10.*)
Rejoicing within,
    The warrior-priests
    Quietly rise and move away.

(BENKEI *moves swiftly down the* HANAMICHI *followed by
the four retainers.* YOSHITSUNE *rises and, with head
bent low, slowly begins to leave the stage. Suddenly
one of the soldiers crosses to* TOGASHI's *side and
whispers in his ear.*)

TOGASHI. (*Rises abruptly.*) What? That porter? (*With
the help of his stage assistant,* TOGASHI *slips the kimono
from his right shoulder, freeing his arm for action. Re-
ceiving his sword from the bearer, he takes two de-
liberate paces forward, and stops, hand poised on the hilt
of his sword in a threatening gesture.*) Stop! Stop, I

say! (*The action now is very rapid,* YOSHITSUNE *stops, and then as if pulled by invisible strings, he backs toward* TOGASHI. *He kneels again in the same position he was in previously, head low and staff held against one shoulder. At the same time,* BENKEI *turns and rushes past the retainers toward the stage but before he can reach* YOSHITSUNE, *the retainers also turn and start toward the stage. They have their hands on their swords ready to draw, thinking their master is discovered. But with viciously twirling rosary and outstretched arms* BENKEI *succeeds in blocking their headlong rush at the very end of the* HANAMICHI.)

BENKEI. No! Rashness will lose it all!

FULL CHORUS.

"Our Lord is suspected!
  Now is the moment
  Between sinking and floating!"
These are their thoughts as they turn.

BENKEI. (*In feigned rage, shakes his head violently and stamps loudly on the floor. He twirls the rosary about his head in a sweeping arc, and crosses in swiftly to* YOSHITSUNE, *attempting to shield him from* TOGASHI'S *searching gaze. FADE MUSIC NO. 10.*) You! Strong One! Why haven't you passed through?

TOGASHI. (*In a fearsome voice.*) Because I have detained him!

BENKEI. Detained him? What for?

TOGASHI. There are those who say he resembles . . . a certain person. That is why I have detained him.

BENKEI. Well? What's strange about that? One person often resembles another! (*Brazening it out.*) *Who* do you think he resembles?

TOGASHI. My soldiers say the Hogan, Yoshitsune. He is to be held for questioning.

BENKEI. The Hogan? The Strong One resembles the *Hogan,* you say? (*Turning on* YOSHITSUNE *in feigned fury.*) This is something to remember a lifetime! Ohhhh! It's unendurable! We'd planned to reach Noto by sun-

down and now, just because of this lagging porter . . .
this has happened! If people begin suspecting you of
being the Hogan on the slightest provocation, you'll be
the cause of the failure of our mission! (*Grinds his teeth
as if in uncontrollable rage.*) The more I think of it the
more despicable you become! (*He growls through
clenched teeth; he leaps in the air and stamps on the
floor.*) You are hateful I say! Hateful! Hateful!!

FULL CHORUS. (*MUSIC CUE NO. 11. To rapid and
excited* SAMISEN *music.*)
Snatching up the Kongo staff,
    He strikes right . . .
    (*Restraining the tears,* BENKEI *raises the staff high,
then strikes his master on the right shoulder. His
whole body jerks as if he himself had been struck.
Once again he raises the staff, hesitates, his face
contorted with grief, then strikes his master on the
left shoulder.*)
He strikes left!
BENKEI. Now, move on, I tell you!
CHORUS LEADER.
He berates him soundly,
    Ordering him to pass through!

(*Shielding his face,* YOSHITSUNE *rises and quickly crosses
up stage right and kneels with his back to the audience, in effect, removing himself from the scene
which follows.*)

TOGASHI. No matter how you plead his case, he shall
not . . .
THE THREE SOLDIERS. . . . pass through! (*The soldiers stand in a resolute row with their hands on their
sword hilts.* YOSHITSUNE'S *retainers reach for their
swords and are about to attack. Still trying to avert a
conflict,* BENKEI *makes an excuse for the retainers'
actions.*)
BENKEI. For you to eye the *oi* box as you do, you're

not guards at all. You must be thieves! (*He strikes the staff loudly on the floor and poses with it threateningly. The retainers surge forward.* BENKEI *quickly uses the staff to block their path.*) Here! Here!

(BENKEI *forces the retainers back once, but they press forward again. He pushes them back a second time, holding them with the staff until they are calmed.* BENKEI *now turns to face* TOGASHI, *holding the staff before him in both hands. The sight of* BENKEI *striking his own master has come as a physical shock to* TOGASHI. *Impressed with* BENKEI's *daring, momentarily he cannot bring himself to act. But now he dismisses such thoughts and resolves to attack.*)

FULL CHORUS. (*Accompanied by full orchestra.*)
"How cowardly it is!
　To draw swords
　Against a lowly porter!"
With such seeming thoughts,
　And god-frightening looks,
　The priests prepared for battle.

(*Slowly the two opposing groups move toward each other until they meet center stage. On each side the men press against their leader.* BENKEI *and* TOGASHI *glare fiercely at each other. Then* TOGASHI *and the soldiers begin to advance. Slowly, deliberately, using the sliding dance step of Noh, they take one, two, three slow-motion strides forward. In unison,* BENKEI *and the retainers take one, two, three strides backward. The two masses of men pivot and surge as one, bound together by their fierce antagonism. Now* BENKEI *summons his last resources and halts* TOGASHI. *Holding the staff before him, he begins to push* TOGASHI *back. The soldiers and the retainers stand aside as* BENKEI *forces* TOGASHI *back step by step to his original position. The implication*

is that TOGASHI *can no longer bring himself to attack
in the face of* BENKEI'S *great display of courage on
behalf of* YOSHITSUNE. BENKEI *has succeeded in pre-
venting first his own men and now* TOGASHI *from
launching an attack. The victory is his. Defiantly he
faces* TOGASHI. *Twirling the rosary, he swings the
staff about his head, and strikes it on the floor. He
raises the staff over his head and poses.* TOGASHI
*poses with his legs spread wide apart and his hand
on the hilt of his sword. They hold their tableau for
a moment. FADE MUSIC NO. 11.*)

BENKEI. If you still think this miserable creature is
the Hogan, then hold him along with the gifts until our
return! Investigate him any way you wish. Or would you
rather I kill him with this now? (*He strikes the staff on
the floor and brandishes it theateningly.*)

TOGASHI. You are too harsh!

BENKEI. Then why do you still doubt us?

TOGASHI. There is the complaint of my soldiers.

BENKEI. (*With grim determination.*) Then I shall kill
him before your own eyes! Will that convince you?

TOGASHI. (TOGASHI *visibly recoils at the thought. He
is caught up in conflicting emotions. He is aghast to think
that* BENKEI *would actually raise his hand against his
own master, an unheard of act in feudal Japan. At the
same time he recognizes this as an act of supreme de-
votion on* BENKEI'S *part and is overwhelmed with ad-
miration. In* BENKEI *he recognizes his moral superior. He
makes his decision.*) Stop! Do not be hasty! Because of
the baseless suspicions of my soldiers you have already
severely beaten this person who . . . is not the Hogan.
My doubts are now dispelled. (*Speaking brusquely to
cover his emotion.*) Quickly now, pass through the
barrier!

BENKEI. (*Continuing the pretense to the end.*) Were
it not for the words of the Great Lord here, I should have

killed you on the spot! You laggard, you've been lucky this time! Don't tempt the Gods again!

TOGASHI. From now on, it is my duty to maintain even stricter guard! (*His stage assistant fixes the sleeve of his kimono.*) Come with me, men!

THE THREE SOLDIERS. Yes, My Lord.

(BENKEI *and* TOGASHI *face each other once more in tableau. The air fairly crackles with emotion.* BENKEI *has succeeded; he knows this, yet cannot show it. For* TOGASHI'S *part, he knows full well who* BENKEI *and* YOSHITSUNE *are, yet he cannot show this. Further, there is the implication that, having failed his own master* YORITOMO, *the honorable course for him now would be to take his own life. He averts his face so the soldiers cannot see his struggle to maintain composure. Just as he is about to give way to tears, he shakes his head, dismissing the thought of death from his mind. He draws himself up to his full height, pivots regally about, kicking out the long trailing ends of his trousers, and strides off the stage.*)

FULL CHORUS. (*MUSIC CUE NO. 12.*)
Taking his soldiers with him,
    The barrier guard enters within the gate.

(TOGASHI *and the soldiers exit through the small door stage left.* BENKEI *looks after them. The music now becomes plaintive and halting in tempo.* YOSHITSUNE'S *hat and* OI *box have been taken by his stage assistant and now he moves to left center stage where he kneels.* BENKEI *slowly moves to center stage right. He kneels facing* YOSHITSUNE, *his head bent in grief. The retainers kneel in a line up stage between the two. They have symbolically passed through the barrier and are now stopping some distance beyond it.*)

YOSHITSUNE. (*He speaks quietly. In spite of their success he seems subdued and melancholy.*) Benkei, you acted with great presence of mind. Indeed no one but you could have succeeded with such a daring plan. Without hesitation you struck me as recklessly as though I were a lowly servant and so saved me. I stand in awe, for having received the divine protection of our patron, Sho Hachiman, the God of War.

FIRST RETAINER. The barrier guard stopped us and we all felt, "Now is the moment to fight for Our Lord's safety!"

SECOND RETAINER. It is a sign that Sho Hachiman is protecting Our Lord. Our trip from here on to Michinoku should be a swift one.

THIRD RETAINER. Yet without the quick thinking of our Priest of Musashi here, it would have been hard to escape.

FIRST RETAINER. We were . . .

ALL FOUR RETAINERS. . . . truly amazed!

BENKEI. (BENKEI'S *head is bent to the floor. He can scarcely speak for remorse.*) The seers have preached that the end of the world is soon at hand. Yet the sun and the moon have not yet fallen from their places in the heavens. Fate has been kind to Yoshitsune also. How grateful we all are. You speak of strategy, but the fact is I have *struck* my own dear Lord. The heavenly reprisals are frightening to contemplate. These two arms which can lift a thousand *kin* are as though benumbed. How wrong I have been! How wrong! (*FADE MUSIC NO. 12.*)

CHORUS LEADER. (*MUSIC CUE NO. 13.*)
How noble, now,
    Even Benkei,
    Who has never given way before,
Finally shed the tears of a lifetime.

(*His whole body shaking with grief,* BENKEI *bows his head and holds his hand before his eyes in the symbolic gesture of weeping.*)

FULL CHORUS.
The Hogan then took his hand.

(*Rising to one knee,* YOSHITSUNE *extends his right hand to* BENKEI *in token of forgiveness.* BENKEI *starts forward as if to accept his master's gesture, then is overcome with the enormity of his crime. He pulls back sharply, flings down his fan, and bows his head once more to the floor in remorse.*)

YOSHITSUNE. (*To see the rock-like* BENKEI *reduced to tears on his behalf, brings home to* YOSHITSUNE *the full misery and the hopelessness of their position. He too raises his hand to his eyes to cover his tears.*) Why should it be? Why should Yoshitsune, nobly born, his whole life spent in devoted service to his brother, end his life as a corpse sinking unheralded beneath the waves of the Western Sea?

BENKEI. (*Picking up his fan, he holds it before him formally and begins to tell the story of* YOSHITSUNE'S *wanderings.*)
Midst mountain places,
    And rock-bound coasts,
    Awake and asleep,
The warrior spends his lonely existence.
        (*FADE MUSIC NO. 13.*)
    FULL CHORUS. (*MUSIC CUE NO. 14. As the chorus takes up the story,* BENKEI *dances its meaning to the accompaniment of a plaintive melody played by the full orchestra. The pace is slow, the mood softly melancholy.*)
The warrior,
    With armor and sleeve-pillow
    As sole companions . . .
        (BENKEI *mimes sleeping, his head cradled on his kimono sleeve.*)
Sometimes,
    Adrift at sea,
    At the mercy of wind and tide . . .

(*He sculls a boat; his open fan flutters overhead as in the wind.*)

Sometimes,
  In mountain fastnesses,
  Where no hoofprint breaks the white snow . . .
      (*The upside-down fan becomes a mountain.*)
While he endures it all,
  From small evening waves of the sea,
  Come whispers of disgrace and banishment.
      (*To emphasize the strength of the thought,*
      BENKEI *draws the string of an imaginary bow.*
      Then he gestures the throwing of a stone, indicat-
      ing that YOSHITSUNE'S *fortunes are being dashed*
      to earth in the same way. For a moment he holds
      a powerful pose, right hand extended, left hand
      over his head. Then he slowly crosses his eyes, ex-
      ecuting a "MIE," *the most expressive type of pose*
      in Kabuki. Two sharp claps of the stage manager's
      HYOSHIGI *sticks emphasize the emotional tension*
      of the moment.)
For three long years past,
  Like the *oniazami* thistle,
  Which has begun to wither and die,
  Covered only by the frost and dew.
How pitiful it is!

(BENKEI *indicates* YOSHITSUNE *with his closed fan. Then he and the four retainers bow low. Straightening up, they cover their eyes to hide their tears.*)

THE FOUR RETAINERS. Quickly now, My Lord, let us withdraw!
FULL CHORUS.
Pulling on each other's sleeves,
  They seem anxious to be on their way.

(*But* BENKEI *does not move. The fan falls from his nerveless fingers, his head sinks to his chest. FADE MUSIC NO. 14.*)

TOGASHI. (*Off stage.*) Wait! Wait a moment! (*As* BENKEI *rises instantly, prepared to meet whatever new challenge may come,* YOSHITSUNE *retires up stage right where he is covered from view by the four retainers.* TOGASHI *and the soldiers enter through the main entrance stage right and cross immediately to their original positions stage left.*) Forgive my abruptness, but I have brought some *sake,* and though it is nothing much, I hope you will drink with me. (*A small cup is placed on a tray before* TOGASHI *by one of the soldiers, and filled. As is the custom,* TOGASHI, *the host, drinks first. Then the cup on the tray is ceremoniously placed before* BENKEI, *who accepts it center stage, kneeling facing the audience. The cup is filled and* BENKEI *looks at it with undiguised pleasure.*)

BENKEI. My kind Lord, I shall drink with you with pleasure!

CHORUS LEADER. (*MUSIC CUE NO. 15. Accompanied by a single* SAMISEN.)

Truly, truly, Benkei understands this gesture.

How can he ever forget,

Having received this cup of human sympathy?

(BENKEI *tosses off the drink in one swallow. In an expansive mood, now that the crisis is past, he laughingly gestures for the lid of the big lacquered cask stage left to be brought to him and filled with wine. Two soldiers do so, then watch in open-mouthed amazement as* BENKEI *buries his face in the lid and downs an enormous draught.* BENKEI *comes up for air, smacks his lips, and then with a sly chuckle points straight to the audience. The soldiers lean forward, straining to see what is out there, and as they do so,* BENKEI *pushes them off balance and they tumble to the floor.* BENKEI *roars with good natured laughter.*)

And now for tales of the past . . .

(*As a kind of counterpoint to* BENKEI'S *actions, the chorus leader tells of an early love affair* BENKEI *once*

had as a priest, obliquely comparing the difficulties he
faced then to the crossing of the barrier now.)
What embarrassment
  my heart
  once met.
Once met
  a woman
  and confusion.
Along the road of confusion,
  this barrier
  once was crossed.
Being crossed,
  yet another, now,
  with difficulty passed.
Ah, to pass the barrier
  of people's eyes
  is difficult to bear.
It is a transient world!
  We never know enlightenment!
  (BENKEI *empties the lid, then gestures for it to be*
  filled once more. The soldiers hesitate, afraid of the
  consequences, but a menacing glare and a roar of
  mock anger quickly convince them which is the
  lesser of the two evils. They fill the lid at once. His
  eyes gleaming with delight, BENKEI *raises the lid to*
  his lips and drains the entire contents in a single,
  breathtaking swallow. The soldiers stand amazed.
  Now slightly tipsy, BENKEI *puts the lid on his head*
  like a hat, and then, as a stage assistant removes the
  lid, he rises unsteadily to his feet to dance, beating
  time with the closed fan. Now the fan is flicked
  open and it becomes a SAKE *cup; it sails in a grace-*
  ful arc across the stage and it is a SAKE *cup floating*
  down a mountain stream.)
  FULL CHORUS.
How amusing,
  Floating the wine cup
  Down the mountain stream.

The swirling water,
   In eddies and currents,
Splashes the sleeves
   Covering the reaching hand.
   (BENKEI *dances his unsteady way along the "river
   bank" after his "*SAKE *cup." He trips, stumbles, al-
   most falls, then at the last moment recovers his balance. Then, the dance over, and his tipsiness gone, he
   retrieves the fan, folds it, and formally turns to face*
   TOGASHI. *MUSIC FADE NO. 15.*)
Now, let us perform a dance!
   BENKEI. In gratitude, I come to offer you wine! (*He
   holds out the open fan to* TOGASHI, *thus symoblizing an
   offering of drink.*)
      TOGASHI. Come, dance for us.
   BENKEI. (*MUSIC CUE NO. 16.* BENKEI *turns to the
   audience and kneels. When he speaks, it is with great
   emotion. The implied meaning is that he,* BENKEI, *re-
   cognizes what* TOGASHI *has done for them, and that he
   wishes to express his gratitude. At the same time, it is
   implied that* TOGASHI *recognizes the true meaning of*
   BENKEI'S *words.*)
Live myriad long years!
   As the turtle dwells
   On the rocks!
Aryu dondo!
   (*As further expression of his gratitude,* BENKEI *now
   rises and performs a dance taken from the Noh drama.
   In the first section of the dance, he circles the stage
   twice with closed fan and three times with fan open,
   as the drums and flute play a lively rhythmic passage.
   This is a standard Noh dance pattern with no par-
   ticular meaning. In the second section, the tempo becomes much slower, and a* SAMISEN *joins the drums
   and flute.* BENKEI *crosses the stage in a triangular
   figure. His foot movements remain the simple sliding
   steps they were in the first section, but his arm movements and gestures with the open fan become in-*

*creasingly complicated. In the third and final section
of the dance, the tempo quickens again and* BENKEI'S
*dancing takes on an infectious, rhythmic quality. In
a gold and red arc the open fan flashes through the air.*
BENKEI *leaps high and stamps loudly on the floor.
With outstretched arms he twirls the long red rosary.
The dance is concluded as he kneels and ceremoniously
closes the fan.*)

FULL CHORUS.
Originally Benkei was the Wandering Priest of Santo.
    As a youth he danced the Ennen dance.

(BENKEI *now performs a short ENNEN dance, a dance
of longevity, traditionally performed by priests. Inasmuch as* BENKEI *was famous in his youth for his
skill in this dance, and inasmuch as* TOGASHI *would
be expected to know this, to dance it now is a
daring and subtle way for* BENKEI *to express his
gratitude. The complex web of recognition is now
complete: both* BENKEI *and* TOGASHI *know that the
other knows, yet neither can acknowledge the fact
directly. At the conclusion of the dance* BENKEI
*kneels again. Once more playing the role, he com-
ments politely on the beauty of the scene where they
have stopped.*)

BENKEI.
The sound of the falling mountain stream,
    Reverberates on the rocks below.
        (*A piercing note is heard from the flute.*)
That which roars is the waterfall!
That which roars is the waterfall!
        FULL CHORUS. (*With full orchestra accompaniment.*)
The waterfall will roar,
    The sun will shine
Let us take our leave
    Of the barrier guards!
        (*As the music reaches a crescendo,* BENKEI *rises*

*and signals the party to leave with a single, sudden
gesture of the fan.* YOSHITSUNE *and the retainers
move swiftly down the* HANAMICHI *and exit at the
rear of the auditorium.*)
So saying, Benkei
Shouldered the *oi* box.
(*Two stage assistants help* BENKEI *into the* OI *box
harness. Then as he moves quickly toward the*
HANAMICHI, TOGASHI *rises, following his progress
with an intent gaze. At the* HANAMICHI, BENKEI
*pauses, and stands with legs spread wide apart, the
staff held over his head in both hands.* TOGASHI *steps
forward a pace, twirls the long sleeve of his kimono
over his left arm, and raises his closed fan high in
the air. This climactic pose is held for a moment.*)
Feeling as though,
They had trod on the tail of a tiger,
And slipped through the jaws of a dragon,
They departed for the Province of Michinoku.

(*FADE MUSIC NO. 16.* BENKEI *moves quickly onto
the* HANAMICHI, *and the curtain is run closed behind him. Again* BENKEI *pauses; all is silence. He
cannot but think of the great sacrifice* TOGASHI *has
made on their behalf. His eyes are drawn back toward the place where* TOGASHI *was a moment ago.
Then his thoughts abruptly return to the many
difficulties still lying ahead. MUSIC CUE NO. 17.
He resolutely faces front. He twirls the staff round
his head, and poses again, eyes crossed in a* "MIE."
Now he begins his famous "flying ROPPO," *or
"moving-in-six-directions-at-once," exit. He remains
poised for a long instant on one leg, bending and
flexing it. Then he makes a powerful leap forward
onto the other leg. Bending and flexing again, he
prepares for the next leap. With a twirl of the staff
he makes another bound, landing on the opposite
leg. Again the bending and flexing, then another*

leap, and another, and another. Faster and faster he goes, arms and legs flashing in all directions. By the time he reaches the end of the sixty-foot HANAMICHI *he is moving at full speed, in prodigious leaps and bounds, a brilliant and theatrical projection of masculine strength. As* BENKEI *disappears from sight through the* AGEMAKU *curtain, the music and clapping of the sticks reach a crescendo, then quickly taper off.* FADE MUSIC NO. 17. *The play ends as it began, with a few minutes of quiet drum and flute music played by the musicians off stage right.* MUSIC FOR CUE NO. 1 CAN BE RE-PEATED HERE.)

THE ZEN SUBSTITUTE

(*MIGAWARI ZAZEN*)
A KABUKI PLAY
By OKAMUKA SHIKO

English adaptation by
JAMES R. BRANDON
TAMAKO NIWA

THE ZEN SUBSTITUTE
(*Migawari Zazen*)

We settle into our seats in the spacious Kabuki theater. The house lights are up full and, unlike a theater in the West, many of the stage lights are already turned on, so the gold and silver front curtain reflecting this brightness glitters dazzlingly before our eyes. (MUSIC CUE NO. 1.)Leisurely drum beats and the clear sound of a flute, coming from the off-stage musician's room (GEZA), drift out to the audience. Then the drum beats quicken, the flute grows louder, and the curtain swiftly rises. We see revealed a setting as simple as the stage is vast. The scenery consists of a buff colored back piece and two side pieces. They are painted to represent a single spreading pine tree flanked by groves of straight green bamboos, set against plain wooden planking. This is the standard Kabuki representation of the Noh stage. Wide slits cut in the scenery stage right enable the off-stage musicians to follow the action of the play. There are two entranceways to the stage. One is stage right, hung with a brightly striped silk curtain. The other is a raised ramp, the famous HANAMICHI *or "flower way" of the Kabuki theater, that runs straight through the audience to the rear of the auditorium and serves as a splendid showcase for the actors' talents. The stage proper is covered with a special dance floor of smoothly polished cypress wood. Its full area is open to view, completely free of any props or set pieces. (FADE MUSIC NO. 1.)*
As the curtain rises we see four singers and three SAMISEN *players (the* SAMISEN *is a three-stringed instrument) in black formal kimono and brown wing-like outer garments seated on a red platform down stage left.*

51

This is the TOKIWAZU *orchestra which provides musical accompaniment throughout the play.*

From off stage right is heard a sharp, resonant clap of the stage manager's HYOSHIGI *sticks signalling that the performance is about to begin. There is a moment's silence. Nothing moves. Then the* TOKIWAZU CHORUS LEADER *reaches down, picks up the closed fan in front of him, and places it across his right knee. Half chanting, half singing, he gravely declaims his lines, his face an unmoving mask.*

CHORUS LEADER.
Public tranquility!
  Domestic concordity!
  Our land lives in peace!
FULL CHORUS. (*The lead* SAMISEN *player strikes an arpeggio. The other singers pick up their fans and join the* CHORUS LEADER, *singing in high, sweet tones. No hint of the irony of their words can be seen in their impassive faces.*)
Peace without!
Peace within!
No outside gale ruffles
  The harmony of the home.
The spread of green matting
  Lies quiet as the sea.
    (*As they finish singing they place their fans again before them on the platform.*)

(*MUSIC CUE NO. 2. To booming drum beats from off stage the striped curtain stage right flies up and* LORD UKYO *enters. He cuts a magnificent figure, in his voluminous court robe of pale blue silk brocade patterned with silver and gold. The enormous sleeves almost sweep the floor; the long trousers, which fold under his feet and trail behind him, swish back and forth as he struts across the stage. In typical* SAMURAI *style, his head is shaven bare, except for a long, lacquered top-knot coming forward almost to his brow. He carries a closed fan in his right hand. His face and hands are a delicate white. It is an imposing facade until we notice the hint of a pixilated smile on his red lips and a touch of the comic in his up-turned, jet black eyebrows. Center stage he faces front and speaks rapidly, buoyantly.*)

LORD UKYO. I live in the outskirts of Kyoto. But, ohhh, I had a fine time out East a while ago. Stayed at a place near Lake Biwa called the Bide-a-while. A girl named Hanako served me. Poured my wine, took care of me . . . you know! Ho ho—you can say a country girl if you like, but what a face! What a figure! Tender words. Warm heart. Why, when she heard I was back the other day, straight way she came to Kyoto to live, right near by in Kitashirakawa. (*A broad smile.*) She writes me all the time, "I miss you. I want to meet you so." But how? That's the problem. My wife, dear old thing, won't bear an instant's separation. Ahh, it's hard! (*FADE MUSIC NO. 2. He sighs.*) But I've just got to meet her, somehow. Hmmmmmm. (*He closes his eyes in concentration.*) Ah! I have it! (*Slaps thigh with fan. A wicked smile spreads over his face.*) Where is the old shrew? (*Fairly hopping with excitement he sharply pivots right, twirls the kimono sleeve over his right arm, points off stage with the fan, and speaks out eloquently.*) Are you there my love? Are you there my sweet? (*Immediately, he kicks out the trailing ends of his trousers and crosses swiftly to left of center, where he faces front waiting for his wife to enter.*)

FULL CHORUS.
His words allure.
    His tones drip sweet.
She comes in
    Joyfully.
They look so like two cooing doves!

But underneath it
   Lies, such lies!
Fickle man!
   Amorous!
There are two sides
   Two sides
   Two sides to the human heart!

(*On the last lines the stage right curtain flies up and* LADY TAMANOI *enters followed by the two maids,* CHIEDA *and* SAEDA. *She wears a kimono of cream and white embroidered with gold. Her long black hair, tied with a simple colored ribbon at the back of the neck, falls down to her waist. Except for her red daubed cheeks, her face is pure white, as are her hands and dancing socks* [TABI]. *Her left arm is extended in front of her in the standard Noh stance, and as she enters, she moves with the rhythmic, gliding steps of Noh dance in which the foot is never raised from the surface of the floor. Around us the audience is tittering. For it is immediately apparent that this lovely exterior belies a veritable monster of a woman. Physically she is huge, as solid as granite. And behind the facade of Japanese feminine submissiveness lies a will of granite to match. Yet for all that, she is a woman, a woman in whom feminine instincts and an iron will are constantly in conflict.*)

LADY TAMANOI. (*She nods ever so slightly in the direction of her husband.*) You called, my dear? What can I do for you?

LORD UKYO. First, come over here beside me a moment. (*He moves dead center. She crosses past him to his left, and the attendants move to his right. They all kneel. The women drape the long left sleeve of their* KIMONO *over their laps.*)

LADY TAMANOI. (*Ever so polite.*) What is it, my dear?

LORD UKYO. Oh, it's nothing, really. I, ah . . . well, I didn't want to worry you, but I've been having nightmares, terrible nightmares the past few nights. I, ah . . . I've been thinking a good pilgrimage might be just the thing to purify my soul. Ha ha! Yes that's it, yes. That's what I wanted to say.

LADY TAMANOI. What do you mean by a pilgrimage? (*Suspicious.*) How long would it take?

LORD UKYO. Yes, well. I've been thinking of visiting different temples . . . all around the country, you see, so, ah, oh, I don't know, it might take a year . . . ha ha ha. . . . (*He fairly gurgles with anticipation, then sees her shocked look. He puts on a forlorn air.*) It might *even* take two years.

LADY TAMANOI. (*Half rising.*) Two years? Oh you can't mean it. It'll break my heart! Chieda, Saeda! Stop him! I won't let him go! (*She beckons them to come.*)

CHIEDA and SAEDA. Yes, my Lady.

(CHIEDA *and* SAEDA *bow with elaborate politeness to their* LADY, *then rise and approach* LORD UKYO. *They pantomime holding his sleeves, but he brusquely shakes them off. They subside to respectful kneeling positions behind him.* LADY TAMANOI *sinks back to the floor on the verge of tears.*)

LORD UKYO. Ha ha, I'm really glad you object; my dear, it shows how much you care for me. You know my love its not that I want to go. Its just these hideous nightmares. I don't see any other way out.

SAEDA. Then at least, to make her happy. . . .

CHIEDA. Can you not perform austerities here at home?

SAEDA and CHIEDA. Yes, my Lord, please do. (*Placing their palms on the floor before them, they bow low.*)

LADY TAMANOI. Is that possible! Can that be done?

SAEDA. Why yes, my Lady.

SAEDA and CHIEDA. Of course, my Lady.

(*MUSIC CUE NO. 3. The* TWO MAIDS *bow, then rise*

and come down center stage where they dance the words of the CHORUS. *At the same time,* LORD UKYO *moves left. He sits on a black lacquered cask brought out for him by a* STAGE ASSISTANT [KOKEN], *in formal dress of the Tokugawa period. The* ASSISTANT *adjusts the folds of* LORD UKYO'S *costume and then retires unobtrusively up stage.* LADY TAMANOI *remains where she is to watch the dance.*)

FULL CHORUS. (*Metallic drum beats from the* KOT-SUTZUMI *drum off stage right punctuate a rhythmic* SAMISEN *accompaniment.*)
From the beginning,
   Twelve roads of escape
Have been known
   To break the wheel of Karma.
And one of these
   Is to submit the flesh
   To austerities.
A million prayers honor the Lord Buddha.
Voices chant the Lotus Sutra.
The beads of the rosary flash and whirl
   Round and round and round.
   (*The girls weave patterns of graceful, supple move-ment. Their arms swing in wide arcs. They kneel and rise. In unison they circle the stage. The sounds of a bass drum and tinkling bells from off stage right mingle with the music of the* TOKIWAZU *orchestra.*)
The deep-booming drum.
The tinkling bell.
The beat of the hollow gourd.
Echo, "Namu Amida Butsu!"
   "All praise the Lord Buddha!"

(*FADE MUSIC NO. 3. Dance finished, the girls tuck their fans in their sashes and retire up stage right where they kneel respec.'ully.*)

CHIEDA. (*Like the* CHORUS, *the sweetness of the girls'*

voices often belies the real meaning of what they say.)
And there are other marvelous austerities as well, my
Lord. There is exposure to the wintry gale, bathing in ice
water, living in total silence. . . .
    SAEDA. . . . moxa burning of the arms, my Lord. . . .
    CHIEDA. . . or of the face, if you prefer.
    SAEDA. So please, my Lord. . . .
    SAEDA and CHIEDA. (*Both bowing low with the utmost
humility.*) . . . consent to perform some simple austerity
here at home.
    LORD UKYO. Ice water? A man of my position? (*Appalled at the thought.*) Never.
    LADY TAMANOI. As you like, but you're not going to
leave this house! (*She fixes him with a determined glare.*)
    LORD UKYO. (*For a few moments he holds his own,
then he turns away.*) Damn! (*His head falls to his chest.
Then he gradually straightens up. Raptly thinking of
Hanako, he rises and unconsciously drifts right until he
is standing directly in front of his wife.*)
    FULL CHORUS.
Wandering heart,
  Amorous heart,
  Hunting Hanako.
    (LORD UKYO *raises his arm, pointing off into the
    distance. His long sleeve blocks* LADY TAMANOI's
    view completely.)
But all our dreams
  Are empty dreams,
  Caught by thorns at home.
    (*In one motion she rises to her knees, sweeps the
    offending sleeve aside, and pops her malevolent face
    into his. His idyllic dream is shattered. He backs off
    distastefully, then sinks to a heap on the floor.*)
Spirits crushed,
  Head bent low,
  He thinks dejectedly:
"What shall I do?"
"What *can* I do?"

LORD UKYO. (*Slaps his thigh with his closed fan and looks up suddenly.*) Ah ha! I have it! (*Turns to his wife.*) My dearest, my sweet, if you really don't want me to go out, all right, I won't. What I'll do is perform a seven day and seven night Zen meditation right here.

LADY TAMANOI. In the family temple?

LORD UKYO. The temple in the garden.

LADY TAMANOI. Ah, that's a good idea. Then I can stay by your side through it all. I'll bring you tea, and I'll bring you hot water. And I'll . . .

LORD UKYO. (*Waving fan at her.*) No, no, no! Woman is evil. In religion I mean. A mere glance from you and my mind would utterly desert Buddha. You must not be there!

LADY TAMANOI. Well, if I'm not going to be there, you aren't either. (*In a sulk she turns her back on him.*)

LORD UKYO. How can you say that? How can you refuse this single small request of mine? Please, my dear. Please, my love. (*He presses his palms together in supplication. He bows meekly to the floor.*)

CHORUS LEADER.
The code of the ancients remains:
    A woman's life is to obey
Three men,
    Her father
    Her husband
    Her son.

FULL CHORUS.
We must advise you not
    CHORUS LEADER.
To tamper with the wisdom of the ages!

CHIEDA. Ohh! See how he implores you, my Lady. He is even bowing before you.

SAEDA. Should you really keep saying, "You can't do this," "You can't do that"?

CHIEDA. It's only to do a little Zen.

SAEDA. Won't you say yes?

SAEDA and CHIEDA. Please say yes, my Lady. (*They bow to the floor.*)

LADY TAMANOI. Hmph! (*She turns to him.*) Well, all right. If you insist, you have my permission. Tonight you may immerse yourself in the spirit of Zen. (*Coldly, she rises and turns to go.*)

LORD UKYO. Tonight? Only one night?

LADY TAMANOI. Did I say two nights?

LORD UKYO. I see. Well, then if that's the way it must be, it's *zazen* tonight, all night.

LADY TAMANOI. Until tomorrow morning, my dear. Early. (*She turns away.*)

LORD UKYO. (*Rising on his knees and gesturing firmly with his fan.*) Remember! You are not to come to see me, you hear. You are not to disturb me when I'm seeking Nirvana.

LADY TAMANOI. I promise. But remember, your meditation is just for one night.

LORD UKYO. Absolutely no visits, my dear! (*He shakes his fan at her then holds that pose.*)

LADY TAMANOI. Positively, one night, my sweet! (*She faces front, and strikes a commanding pose. For a moment they both freeze in a* MIE, *a tableau expressive of their violent opposition.*)

FULL CHORUS.
She bestows her
　Gracious consent!

(*She breaks the tableau and starts to go off right. Suddenly she remembers something and stops. She throws him a haughty look over her shoulder. Instantly he executes an elaborate bow, touching his head to the floor. He holds this humiliating position as a flicker of satisfaction crosses her usually stern face. Now she turns slightly toward the attendants, and they too bow obediently to the floor. Mollified, she sweeps grandly off stage right. CHIEDA and SAEDA rise and follow in her wake. The instant they are through the doorway,* LORD UKYO *leaps to his feet.*)

LORD UKYO. (*Alone, his personality changes completely. He lets out a boisterous laugh.*) Ho ho! I fooled her, I fooled her, didn't I. She's clever that one, but after all only a woman! ha ha! Now where's that Taro. (*With a flourish of trouser ends he turns and calls off right.*) Heh, Taro! Tarooooooooooo! (*Without waiting for any response, and bubbling with good spirits, he swiftly strides stage left.*)

TAROKAJA. (*Skittering on in a great rush.*) Yes, my Lord.

LORD UKYO. (*In mid stride.*) It's you, Taro?

TAROKAJA. Yes, my Lord.

LORD UKYO. You're here?

TAROKAJA. Yes, sir.

LORD UKYO. You're really here.

TAROKAJA. (*With a little bow.*) Before you, sir.

LORD UKYO. Well what do you know. (*Turns to him with face beaming.*) You're fast today, Taro.

TAROKAJA. And you, my Lord, seem happy today.

LORD UKYO. With good reason, Taro. With good reason. Ho ho! What do you think. (*Moves in close to* TAROKAJA. *Confidentially.*) I got the night off! The whole night, and I'm going to see Hanako!

TAROKAJA. Oh, that's wonderful, sir! (*He begins to laugh, then quickly catches himself.*) How did you manage that, sir?

LORD UKYO. Well, you know the dear shrew. (TAROKAJA *nods.*) She'd never just give me the night off. So I gave her this cock-and-bull story about nightmares and how I had to do *zazen* all night to cleanse my soul.

TAROKAJA. Ohh, that was clever, sir!

LORD UKYO. Yes, wasn't it! I thought so, too. Now, Taro, there's just one thing I want you to do for me.

TAROKAJA. (*Bows respectfully.*) Yes, my Lord.

LORD UKYO. I forbade her, absolutely, to come med-

dling around while I'm in Nirvana. But you know the
kind of old busy-body she is. (*One conspirator to another.*) Sure enough, in the middle of the night, she'll
come sneaking through the bushes to spy on me. And if
she doesn't see someone in meditation she'll be fit to be
tied. Now I know it may be a bit uncomfortable, Taro,
but its only till morning. How about you taking my place
and being religious tonight?

TAROKAJA. (*Swallows hard and bows very respectfully.*) Of course, anything for my Lord. But please sir,
not this.

LORD UKYO. Ehhh? (*Commandingly.*) What's this?

TAROKAJA. Sir! Its your wife's. . . . terrible temper.

(*MUSIC CUE NO. 4.* TAROKAJA *bows low to* LORD UKYO,
*then moves down stage and faces the audience. As
the* CHORUS *sings, he mimics* LADY TAMANOI *in
dance-pantomime. His movements are half-feminine,
half-loutish.*)

FULL CHORUS. (*Off-stage drums punctuate the* SAMISEN
melody.)
The dear thing loves you so,
    When you're at home
    Her face is wreathed in smiles.
        (*Kneeling before an imaginary mirror,* TAROKAJA
        *coyly adjusts the hang of his kimono. He pats pow-
        der on his beaming face.*)
Her chubby cheeks glow
    And burst with joy
    Like eternally smiling Otafuku.
        (*Rising,* TAROKAJA *puffs out his cheeks, mocking
        the looks of* OTAFUKU, *the overweight Goddess of
        Happiness. Angry and amused at the same time,*
        LORD UKYO *reprimands* TAROKAJA *by tapping him
        smartly on the forehead with his fan.* TAROKAJA *is
        undaunted, but he at least makes an attempt to hide
        his mirth, as he turns away and continues his dance.*)

But when she's angry,
  She's a raving demon.
And when she hates
  She's a witch!
  A fiend!
  A devil!
Like a gargoyle perched on a rain spout!
If she ever finds out
  About a trick like this!
  This Taro's as good as dead!
      (TAROKAJA *cowers, then beats himself wildly on the*
      head with both hands. Finally he sinks in a heap to
      the floor as if dead. His act finished, he bows.)
So excuse me just this once, he said.
  He begged.
  He bowed.
  He implored.
      (*FADE MUSIC NO. 4.*)
  LORD UKYO. (*He has had enough nonsense. He tucks*
the fan under the collar of his kimono and steps forward
threateningly.) So! You're afraid of her but not of me!
Eh Taro? That mistake will cost you your head! (*He*
rears back, stamps, and grasps the hilt of his sword. Legs
wide apart, arms akimbo, he poses for a moment without
moving.)
  TAROKAJA. (TARO *throws up his hands to ward off the*
blow.) No, no, no, my Lord! Wait! (*There is good reason*
for TAROKAJA *to be afraid, for in feudal Japan it was*
a SAMURAI'S *prerogative to kill on the spot any commoner*
who opposed his will.) I was wrong. My Lordship is the
frightening one. I shall do whatever you say. (*He bows*
low, but almost immediately pops up again, as he realizes
he is presenting an inviting target for his master's
sword.)
  LORD UKYO. (*Without moving.*) You're sure of that,
Taro?
  TAROKAJA. Yes, my Lord!
  LORD UKYO. Truthfully?

THE ZEN SUBSTITUTE 63

TAROKAJA. Yes, yes, my Lord.
LORD UKYO. (*Turns his head slightly to hide a smile he can't completely suppress.*) Positively?
TAROKAJA. (*Frantic, he bows again and again.*) Yes sir! Yes sir!
LORD UKYO. (*With a hearty laugh he drops his pose and crosses center.*) Then I won't kill you today. It was only a joke, Taro.
TAROKAJA. It was a bad joke, sir.
LORD UKYO. Sometimes you need a good frightening. Now here. Sit. (*A STAGE ASSISTANT has brought a black lacquered cask about two feet high to just left of center stage. LORD UKYO motions for TAROKAJA to sit, and TAROKAJA does so. The STAGE ASSISTANT hands LORD UKYO a folded silk robe.*) On with the robe. (*LORD UKYO and the STAGE ASSISTANT drape the robe of golden silk over TAROKAJA's head. The STAGE ASSISTANT kneels behind the cask, where he remains unobtrusively throughout most of the remainder of the play.*)
CHORUS LEADER.
A brilliant colored robe,
    Hides the seated form.

(*LORD UKYO circles TAROKAJA. He examines the robe from all angles, carefully adjusting a fold here, a drape there. He returns center stage, and stands back a few paces, the better to survey his handiwork.*)

LORD UKYO. Perfect. From the front, the side, the back, you'd never know it wasn't me.
TAROKAJA. (*He pops his head out.*) I think Zen meditation is just a fancy way of saying torture, my Lord. I can tell it already.
LORD UKYO. Be brave! It's only one night. (*Glances fearfully off in the direction of his wife, then tiptoes up to TAROKAJA. Confidentially.*) Remember. If she shows up keep the robe on and you'll be all right.

TAROKAJA. Yes sir.

LORD UKYO. And whatever you do, God help you don't open your mouth.

TAROKAJA. Yes sir.

LORD UKYO. (*Glowing with anticipation.*) Well then. I'm off.

TAROKAJA. Hurry back, sir. Please, sir!

LORD UKYO. Goodbye! (*He turns and starts to go off.*)

TAROKAJA. Goodbye!

LORD UKYO. Goodbye!

TAROKAJA. Goodbye!

BOTH. (*Their alternate "goodbyes" rhythmically increase in speed until they are speaking as rapidly as possible and finally in unison.*) Goodbye, goodbye, goodbye, goodbye, goodbye, goodbye, goodbye!

TAROKAJA. Just a moment, sir! (LORD UKYO *stops down stage right, before the* HANAMICHI. TAROKAJA *rises, and crosses to his master. The robe falls to his shoulders.*) Excuse me, sir, I know it's a bother, but . . . when you get to Lady's Hanako's, would you please say hello to her for me? To Kobai, her maid?

LORD UKYO. Hehhh? You mean you and Kobai? While I was . . . (TAROKAJA *nods happidly.* LORD UKYO *bursts out in delighted laughter.*) Ha ha ha!

TAROKAJA. (*Rythmically repeating the laughter.*) Ha ha ha!

LORD UKYO. (*Pokes* TAROKAJA *playfully in the chest with his closed fan.*) Ho ho ho!

TAROKAJA. Then you will say hello for me, sir?

LORD UKYO. Of course, I . . . (*Suddenly catches himself.*) Here now, what kind of Zen meditation is this? Are you trying to walk to Nirvana? (*He stamps his foot in mock anger and shoos* TAROKAJA *back to the cask.*) Sit, sit, sit, sit! And meditate! (*He carefully scrutinizes the covered form as the* STAGE ASSISTANT *adjusts the folds of the robe on all sides.*) Now, not a word. I'm off.

TAROKAJA. (*Peeping out sadly.*) I'll be waiting, sir. Hurry back, please.

LORD UKYO. (*Happy as a lark, he moves right toward the* HANAMICHI.) Goodbye.
TAROKAJA. Goodbye.
LORD UKYO. Goodbye.
BOTH. (*Same rhythmic speaking as before.*) Goodbye, goodbye, goodbye, goodbye, goodbye, goodbye!

(*Just as he is about to step onto the* HANAMICHI, LORD UKYO *stops and casts one last glance at the forlorn huddled figure center stage. Free at last, he sighs; a fatuous grin covers his round face. As the* CHORUS *sings, he moves with simpering dance steps onto the* HANAMICHI.)

FULL CHORUS.
Into the night,
Into the mists,
"Goodbye, goodbye!"
Heedless of eyes,
Heedless of gossip,
Away, away!
Wet by dew,
And the warmth of love,
He dreams, he dreams.

(LORD UKYO *pauses for a moment on the* HANAMICHI. *He smiles a love-sick smile and bashfully lowers his eyes. Then he charges into action: he straightens up, stamps loudly on the floor, whirls the long kimono sleeve around his right arm with a great flourish and points off down the* HANAMICHI *with trembling fan.*)

LORD UKYO. (*Half elf, half devil.*) Whee! I'm off at last! Going, going, going, going, *gone!* (*He races delightedly down the* HANAMICHI *and whisks out of sight. The striped* AGEMAKU *curtain flies closed after him.*)
TAROKAJA. (*In time with the departure of* LORD UKYO, TAROKAJA *pokes his head out from under the robe.*

Watching his master disappear into the distance he rises and drifts unconsciouly toward the HANAMICHI.) Come back soon, sir. While she doesn't know. Please sir! And give my love to Kobai. . . . won't you . . . sir . . . *(He gazes off forlornly, in silence.)* What am I doing! Talking during *zazen! (He crosses hurriedly back and sits on the cask. The* STAGE ASSISTANT *drapes the robe over his head.* TAROKAJA *holds the collar of the robe straight out in front of him with both arms extended. As long as he doesn't drop his arms the audience can see every expression of his face.)* How uncomfortable! What a bore! *(He groans, then lapses into silence.)*

FULL CHORUS.
An empty robe,
    A husk remains.
        (The curtain stage right flies up and LADY TAMANOI *enters.)*
Her heart goes out to him—
    Poor, lonely soul
Performing his act of piety.

LADY TAMANOI. *(She comes down stage, right of center, and faces the audience. As before, her left arm is extended in Noh dance style.)* Imagine, the poor dear, sitting out in the cold all night long, thinking about Buddha. All alone. What a terrible ordeal. How can I keep away? I must see his sweet, suffering form. *(She takes a halting step toward him, symbolic of crossing through the garden toward him. She cocks her head quizzically in his direction. Her hand flutters to her massive breast. She staggers back a pace, and looks beseechingly at the audience.)* Oh, he looks so miserable! It's even worse than I thought. I can't stand it. I've got to help him. Chieda! Saeda! Bring the food at once as I told you. *(She lumbers frantically right gesticulating distractedly to the* TWO MAIDS *off stage.)* Hurry! Hurry! Hurry! *(*TAROKAJA *peeks out and sees the dread form of* LADY TAMANOI. *He begins to shake violently with fright, then ducks quickly back under the robe as the* TWO

MAIDS *enter,* CHIEDA *carrying a small black lacquered tray piled with cakes and* SAEDA *carrying one with a cup of ceremonial tea.* LADY TAMANOI *kneels respectfully to* TAROKAJA'S *right, the* MAIDS *kneel behind her.*) I know I promised not to come, but you looked so pathetic. Let me serve you a cup of wine. It will strengthen your religious resolve. (*The robe nods vigorously a few times, then suddenly reverses itself and shakes "no."* TAROKAJA *pulls the robe tightly around him.*) No? Then at least have some tea. (*The robe shakes "no" again.* LADY TAMANOI *beckons to* CHIEDA *and* SAEDA *to bring the cakes and tea. They approach* TAROKAJA, *kneel directly in front of him, bow low, and place the two trays at his feet. They bow again, rise gracefully and glide back across the stage to their usual positions up stage right.*)

CHORUS LEADER.
Surely Buddha can't begrudge
  Such selfless
  Generosity!
FULL CHORUS.
Imploring him, urging him!
LADY TAMANOI. Just a cup of tea, my Lord, only a cup of tea.

(TAROKAJA *shakes his head vigorously, but he doesn't let out a peep.*)

CHORUS LEADER. (*MUSIC CUE NO. 5. To the singing of the* CHORUS LEADER *and slow* SAMISEN *music,* LADY TAMANOI *rises and dances.*)
This is too much!
  This is too much!
You tread the path,
  You seek the light
  Of eternal Buddahood.
Ignoring me, your dear sweet wife
  Who serves you here
  And now. . . .

Are you really more the man, more pure this way?
(LADY TAMANOI *determines to take matters into her own hands and put an end to her husband's misery. She beckons* CHIEDA *to come over and take the robe off the seated figure.* CHIEDA *does not move. Even after* LADY TAMANOI *pulls her to her feet and pushes her center stage she politely refuses. She is not getting mixed up in anything as unpleasant as a scrap between her Lord and her Lady. When* LADY TAMANOI *tries to take the robe off herself,* CHIEDA *first blocks her path, and then holds her back by force by grasping the broad sash of her Lady's kimono. Actions that might be violent are muted; physical contact is portrayed symbolically; they move slowly, with graceful, stylized motions. At the end of the dance,* CHIEDA *moves stage right.* LADY TAMANOI *stands for a moment irresolute.*)
Sightless eyes,
　Wordless lips,
　He holds to Buddha's way.
Tear soaked eyes.
　Blubbering lips,
　Yes, this is woman's way!
(*For the moment at least, feminine tenderness asserts itself.* LADY TAMANOI *falls clumsily to her knees. Her huge bulk heaves up and down in passionate sobs. Her right hand covers her eyes, in the symbolic gesture of weeping that is almost touching in its attempt at daintiness.*)
And in the end,
　Happily
　She nuzzles up to him.

(*She minces over to his side, kneels, and rests her head coquettishly on his thigh. When he doesn't respond, except for shudders, she grasps his knee and violently shakes him, rather like a playful St. Bernard with a rag doll.* TAROKAJA'S *only response is to shudder all the more.*)

LADY TAMANOI. At least then, a glimpse of your precious face, my love.

(*The* SAMISEN *music quickly increases in tempo. The* TWO MAIDS *approach. The* STAGE ASSISTANT *whisks away the two trays and places them safely up stage. The terror stricken* TAROKAJA *takes one quick look at the three of them descending on him and ducks back under the robe. Scrunching down as far as he can, he pulls the robe tightly around his frail quaking body.* LADY TAMANOI *on his right and the* TWO MAIDS *on his left, pull the robe first one way, then the other. Desperately he holds it fast. His feet beat out a nervous tattoo on the floor. Pulling harder and harder, the women lift him to his feet. The* STAGE ASSISTANT *snatches the cask out of their way. The women whirl him around in a circle once, then again.*)

FULL CHORUS.
They pull, he tugs,
   They jostle, he struggles!
   Round and round they go!
In a flash it's off!
A thunderbolt!
It's only Tarokaja!

(*As the robe flies off,* CHIEDA *and* SAEDA *flee up stage right.* TAROKAJA *gasps, and falls prostrate to the floor.*)

LADY TAMANOI. (*She stamps thunderously on the resonant dance floor. The words pour out in a torrent.*) It's you? You? You wretch! Where did he go? Where did he go? Where did you let him go?
   TAROKAJA. I . . . I . . . I . . .
   LADY TAMANOI. Answer me! Answer meeeee!
   TAROKAJA. (*Trying to stem the tide.*) He went to Lady Hanako's. He went to Lady . . .

LADY TAMANOI. Lady? You dare say *Lady?* Say hussy!
Say hussyyyyy! (She stamps viciously for emphasis.)
TAROKAJA. Yes, hussy. Hussy, hussy, hussy, hussy,
hussy, hussy! He made me wear the robe so he could
slip away. (*He bobs up and down in pathetic little bows.*
LADY TAMANOI *wrings the robe as if it were* TAROKAJA's
*neck, and fixing him with a murderous gaze, step by step
begins to advance on him. Half kneeling, half duck-
walking he edges away. In time to* SAMISEN *music they
move in unison, she advancing, he retreating: a cobra
and its hypnotized prey. They make a half circle of the
stage until they have exactly changed positions. She is
now stage left, he stage right. FADE MUSIC NO. 5.*
TAROKAJA *bows low.*) I couldn't help it. It wasn't my
fault. He drew his sword, my Lady. Don't kill me,
madam. Please. (*He bows again, then sensing he is
getting no response from* LADY TAMANOI, *he scrambles
to his feet and dashes over to the* TWO MAIDS.) Saeda,
Chieda. Help get me off. Apologize for me. You know
how. (*He takes* SAEDA *by the arm and tries to drag her
center. In dance motions they struggle back and forth
for a moment, then she escapes.* TAROKAJA *pulls* CHIEDA
*to her feet and tries to lead her center. She pushes him
into* SAEDA, *who in turn gives him another push. He
stumbles across the stage, off balance. Just as he is about
to crash into* LADY TAMANOI, *he regains his balance. Immediately he prostrates himself before her.*)
FULL CHORUS.
The usually light-hearted Taro,
    Cowers in craven fear,
    Before here ever more violent rage.
He grovels,
    Begging forgiveness.
LADY TAMANOI. You mean he actually said he'd kill
you if you didn't obey?
TAROKAJA. (*Bowing low.*) Oh yes, my Lady, he did.
LADY TAMANOI. (*Wavering between hurt and anger.*)
Hmph! Why didn't he tell me the truth straight out,

that he wanted to see this Hanako creature. For one night, I'd have let him go. Maybe. But no, he tried to make a fool of me. (*She shakes the robe in a fury, then throws it to the floor and stamps violently. The* STAGE ASSISTANT *scurries forward to retrieve the robe, folds it, and retires up stage.*) A fool of me! A fool of meeeeeeeee . . . . . . (*Her cry of rage dissolves into sobs. She sinks to her knees, blubbering.*) . . . eehee. . . . eehee. . . . eehee. . . .

CHIEDA. Such an evil master.

SAEDA. So very evil lately.

(*They bow to the floor.*)

LADY TAMANOI. Oh, Taro, please be my friend. You've honestly confessed and so I've decided to forgive you . . . on one condition.

TAROKAJA. Oh, thank you, my Lady! Anything.

LADY TAMANOI. I'm going to take your place. I want you to cover me with the robe, just the way he covered you.

TAROKAJA. But . . . but . . . my Lady, he'll kill me when he finds out!

LADY TAMANOI. You said anything.

TAROKAJA. (*Swallowing hard.*) Anything but this. Oh, please!

LADY TAMANOI. You're afraid of him then, but not of me? (*She rises abruptly, stamps twice on the floor and poses in a blood-chilling* MIE. *Face twisted in anger, arms cocked threateningly, fingers stretched like claws, hair falling across her shoulders, she looks like some kind of witch.*) You will do as I say, if you value your life! (*She fixes him with a malevolent glare.*) Or shall I kill you? (*She makes a sudden move, and* TAROKAJA *throws his hands up to ward off the blow.*)

TAROKAJA. Oh, no, no, no! Whatever you say. Anything for my life.

LADY TAMANOI. (*Spitting it out.*) Then do it now! Quickly! Quickly, I say!

TAROKAJA. Yes, madam. Yes, madam. (*He bows repeatedly. He and the* MAIDS *rise and quickly cross center stage to carry out her orders.*)

LADY TAMANOI. (*Fluttering with excitement.*) Faster, faster, faster!

(*The* STAGE ASSISTANT *places the lacquered cask where it was before.* LADY TAMANOI *plumps herself down on it, stamping and fuming all the while, urging them on.* TAROKAJA, *to her left, and the* TWO MAIDS, *to her right, take the robe from the* STAGE ASSISTANT, *unfold it, and drop it over her head.*)

FULL CHORUS.
The maids and Taro
  Drape the robe.
They adjust its folds.
  Then back away.

(*The* MAIDS *retire up stage right. Just as his master did,* TAROKAJA *inspects the robe first on the left side, then on the right. He kneels and bows respectfully.*)

TAROKAJA. My Lady, you look his exact image, believe me. Like two peas in a pod.

SAEDA. The very image.

CHIEDA. Indistinguishable.

(*The* TWO MAIDS *bow.*)

LADY TAMANOI. (*She lifts the robe a bit. We see a beaming face.*) I *do* look like him then? Oh, splendid, splendid! Now as long as he doesn't see any of you he'll never suspect. Humph, I suppose you're tired, Taro?

TAROKAJA. Thank you, my Lady, thank you.

LADY TAMANOI. All right. You can all go now.

ALL. (*Bowing respectfully.*) Yes, my Lady.

(TAROKAJA *is the first to rise. He tiptoes cautiously right,
half expecting to be called back. When he reaches
the exit and realizes he is safe, he lets out a sigh of
relief. He turns for one last look at* LADY TAMANOI
*huddled under the robe. The delightful irony of the
scene to come flashes through his mind. He turns his
smirking face full front, sharing with the audience
his unconcealed delight at the situation. Then,
smothering his laughter as best he can, he dashes
off right.* CHIEDA *and* SAEDA *demurely rise and
follow.*)

FULL CHORUS.
The three of them bow . . .
   CHORUS LEADER.
. . . quietly rise . . .
   FULL CHORUS.
. . . and leave the room.

(*For a moment all that can be seen on the wide stage
are the impassive faced musicians far stage left and
a shimmering spot of gold in the center. There is
a moment of silence; nothing moves. Then at a
signal from the* STAGE MANAGER, *a single sharp clap
of the* HYOSHIGI *sticks, the second section of
MIGAWARI-ZAZEN begins. MUSIC CUE NO. 6.
From back stage comes the sound of measured drum
beats and the rising wail of a flute, soon joined by
the sonorous strumming of many* SAMISEN. *In a moment the source of this music is revealed. The back-
drop of straight bamboos and the gnarled pine
swiftly rises revealing a* NAGAUTA, *or "long-song"
orchestra, seated in two rows against an identically
painted scene of bamboos and pine. In the top row
sit eight* SAMISEN *players and eight singers; in the
bottom row sit seven musicians who play, in order
from left to right, a flute* [YOKOBUE], *three shoulder-
drums* [KOTSUZUMI], *a hip-drum* [TSUZUMI], *and*

two small standing drums [TAIKO]. *The identical jet black kimono and powder blue winged outer garments which the singers and musicians wear, stand out vividly against the scarlet draped two-level platform. The acting area has been considerably deepened and twenty-three more people have been added to the stage, but as the new scenery is exactly like the old, and as the change was carried out in a twinkling, the eye is scarcely aware of any change at all. The singers bend forward to pick up their fans, place them across their right knees, and begin to sing.)*

FULL NAGAUTA CHORUS. (*With flute and drum accompaniment.*)
How wonderful!
  To loosen her silken gown!
How glorious!
  Down to the inner sash!
NAGAUTA CHORUS LEADER. (*A slow, plaintive melody.*)
He ambles home tipsily, hair
  Awry
  Mussed
  And tumbled.
Hanging dishevelled
  Like weeping
  Willow strands.
(LORD UKYO'S *appearance at the end of the* HANAMICHI *is greeted with laughter and scattered applause. He has exchanged his fancy blue robe for a knee-length, black, silk outer garment tied at the waist with a pink sash. In a happy fog of dreams and alcohol, and humming to himself, a self-satisfied smile spread across his moon-face, he staggers into sight and begins to dance his weaving, eccentric way down the* HANAMICHI *toward the stage. His comic actions are in marked contrast to the sentimentality of the accompanying* NAGAUTA *song.*)
Her fragrance clings
  Still to his sleeve.

Her image yet
  To his heart.
LORD UKYO. (*FADE MUSIC NO. 6. Still on the*
HANAMICHI, *near the stage, he shuffles to a stop suddenly
overcome by melancholy. He looks back and points long-
ingly into the distance with his closed fan. His eyes mist
over; when he speaks his tongue is thick and slow.*) She
came with me a long, long way. But when I looked back,
where her visage once stood, there lingered only a sliver
of a moon. (*The fan drops from his nerveless fingers; he
lurches forward a step.*)
  TOKIWAZU FULL CHORUS. (*MUSIC CUE NO. 7. Ab-
ruptly the orchestra switches to a lively tune.* LORD
UKYO's *cheerful mood returns, and flipping open his red
and gold fan, he begins to dance. He twirls around on
one leg; trouser ends and dangling hair fly through the
air. Tipsy and gay, he prances about.*)
In the beginning,
  A lover's quarrel,
Soon glossed over,
  By drinking and singing.
Relenting finally
  She offered her robe.
The time to take his leave
  Came all too soon.
(*Again the music becomes plaintive, lingering.* LORD
UKYO's *touseled head sinks to his chest, his arms hang
loose.*)
We see in the scattered remnants of a cloud,
  A reminder of this morning's parting.
  TOKIWAZU CHORUS LEADER.
Splay-footed and staggering. . . .
  LORD UKYO. Ah, at last. (*He lurches to a sudden stop,
and belches decorously.*)
  TOKIWAZU CHORUS LEADER.
. . . he weaves his way,
  Virtuously home.
  LORD UKYO. (*Regally he draws himself up, he slaps*

*his thigh with the closed fan in a gesture of lofty re-
solution. He stamps once and whirls to face the stage.
Then, as if it is just too difficult to maintain, he drops
the high-and-mighty pose, and with mincing gait toddles
onto the stage proper. FADE MUSIC NO. 7. Seeing the
robed figure of "*TAROKAJA*" he stops, turns, and speaks
directly to the audience.*) Isn't it good to be master of
someone else! There he sits. Just as I ordered. Absolutely
miserable! (*He laughs delightedly. On tiptoe, he gingerly
approaches "*TAROKAJA*," and pokes "him" with his fan.*)
Psst. Heh, Taro. I'm back. Psst! Did the old biddy come?
(*As* LADY TAMANOI *flashes bolt upright, we see her
shocked and outraged face. Then she whips the robe
down over her face once more and shakes it "no."*) She
didn't? (*The robe shakes "no" again.* LORD UKYO *can
hardly believe the good news.*) What luck. Ah! It was
wonderful tonight, Taro. Wonderful. How about you?
Was it a bad night? (*The robe shakes "no."*) It wasn't
too uncomfortable? Good fellow! Good fellow! You
know, I think it's true what they say about love: what's
inside shows on the outside. And that's just what I'm
afraid of. When I think of tonight . . . why, if she were
even to catch a glimpse of my face . . . (*He giggles.*)
But you're the only one around here, aren't you, Taro?
So you be a good fellow and listen to my story, eh? (*The
robe nods.*) You will listen? (*Again the robe nods.*) But
first, let's get rid of that ridiculous robe. (*He puts his
hand on her head and is about to take off the robe. She
jerks away so violently he is knocked off balance.*) Oh,
of course, I see. You'd be embarrassed, wouldn't you . . .
Taro? (*He hides his face behind his open fan, and simpering, moves a few steps to the right.*) And I'd be embarrassed, too! (*She glares at him from the robe and shakes
it in anger. Just as he turns back, she pulls the robe
closed.*) Then I'll tell you just as you are. Right? Right.
(*The robe nods.* LORD UKYO *then steps forward formally,
if tipsily, and speaks directly to the audience, slowly and
deliberately.*) First, I approached her domicile. Second,

I drew near and went knock, knock, knock at her door. *(Following the words, he strikes the back of his outstretched left hand with the closed fan. Then placing the fan on the floor before him, he kneels. Instantly, a* STAGE ASSISTANT *approaches him from behind and helps him slip his right shoulder out of the black outer robe, freeing his arm for the dance movements to come.)*

TOKIWAZU CHORUS LEADER. (*MUSIC CUE NO. 8. One* SAMISEN *plays a bitter-sweet melody.*)
The nightingale's call
    Echoes in the depths of the valley.
Sighing her welcome,
    Hanako opens the door.

*(*LORD UKYO *now dance-mimes the full story of their meeting as sung by the* CHORUS, *acting out both his own role and Hanako's. He begins by pantomiming Hanako's actions in graceful linked movements, as "she" bows in welcome, covers her face demurely with her open fan, and takes his hand to lead him into the room.)*

NAGAUTA CHORUS LEADER. (*Full* SAMISEN *accompaniment, with drums and flute. A delicate melody.*)
Scent laden breezes
    Drift through the blinds.
Awakened affection wells
    And flows from her heart.
Spontaneous love is a gift freely given!

(Arching her back, her fan sweeping in an arc overhead, "Hanako" swings back the blinds. She kneels and coyly bows. He returns the bow gallantly, but the blood rushes to his head, and he topples over on his face giddily, trouser ends flying through the air. Next, Hanako lights a pipe for him, a traditional gesture of welcome by geisha and others, and passes it to him ever so politely. He accepts the pipe in a

lordly manner. For the actor it is a genuine tour de force to alternate dancing these two totally different characters. For the audience the quick shifts back and forth between the extroverted, drunken Lord and the coquettish, winsome girl are a source of great amusement. LORD UKYO *puffs contentedly on the pipe a few times before* LADY TAMANOI *explodes in a tantrum of stamping and robe shaking.*)

LORD UKYO. You be quiet! Now listen! (*With a fatuous grin.*) Then the sweet creature looked into my eyes and said reproachfully . . .
TOKIWAZU CHORUS LEADER. (*To the accompaniment of four* SAMISEN.)
My pleading letter
   Brings no reply,
My tearful entreaties
   No visit.
Is my letter discarded?
Am I forgotten?

(*Hanako kneels, opens her fan and writes on it with an imaginary brush. She rolls the fan closed as if it were a letter scroll. Hand pressed to her breast, her heart is breaking; hand to her eyes, she is weeping. The music increases in tempo. Rising, she mimes ripping the fan to shreds then throws it indignantly to the ground.*)

TOKIWAZU FULL CHORUS. (SAMISEN *accompaniment.*)
From silken robes
   Peers forth
Her tear-stained face,
   A rosy flower touched by dew.

(LORD UKYO'S *dance depicts the sadness of the tremulous deserted lover, the effect only slightly marred by a sudden belch.*)

NAGAUTA FULL CHORUS. (*Drums and flute only.*)
Yet see how far
    He comes to see you
    Soaked in the evening's rain.
Can you be bitter?
    Can you threaten him
    With womanly tears?

(*The open fan flutters to the floor, symbolizing the falling
rain. Haughtily, she shakes off his advances; she
brushes the rain drops from her sleeves.*)

TOKIWAZU FULL CHORUS. (*The four* SAMISEN *of the*
TOKIWAZU *orchestra are joined by the drums of the*
NAGAUTA *orchestra.*)
Her pouting face mirrors
    A heart
    Unwarmed by love.
    (*She turns a cold shoulder.*)
But soon he melts
    Her shield of anger
    With tender smiles and laughter.
LORD UKYO. (*FADE MUSIC NO. 8.*) After that, we
went inside and we . . . (*He chuckles tipsily at the
happy memory of what happened next.*) She slipped off
her robe and presented it to me. (*He begins to loosen
the pink sash. A* STAGE ASSISTANT *comes forward and
helps him take off the black robe.* LORD UKYO *gathers it
up and hugs it fondly, thinking of Hanako.* LADY TA-
MANOI *stamps wildly on the floor.*) I said be quiet and
listen! (*Beaming in recollection.*) Then we drank a bit
and we ate a bit. And we talked. And we talked, and we
talked. And we sang, oh yes, we sang, and we danced.

(*The* STAGE ASSISTANT *disappears into the wings with
the black robe. As the* TOKIWAZU *music begins,* LORD
UKYO *sinks to his knees and mimes playing the*
SAMISEN, *all the while happily bouncing up and
down in complete enjoyment.*)

TOKIWAZU FULL CHORUS. (*MUSIC CUE NO. 9. A rhythmic melody played by four* SAMISEN *plus the* NAGAUTA *drums.*)
Through the night we shared
  Untold joys
  And pleasures.
The dawn came all too soon,
  Before we had exhausted
  Our store of talk.
(LORD UKYO *dances playfully over and lets his hand drop heavily on the robed figure. His hand is rudely shaken off.*)
In the grove the early morning birds,
  Warned us
  Of the time.
(LORD UKYO *returns stage right, grotesquely flapping his arms. Because of his long sleeves and trailing trousers, he does present a certain resemblance to a bird, a mad bird, in flight.*)
We rose. I made
  An early farewell.

(LORD UKYO *mimes a grandiloquent farewell.*)

NAGAUTA FULL CHORUS.
She tugged at my sleeve,
  "You cannot go!"

(*"Hanako" puts her kimono sleeves to her eyes to stem the flow of tears, then tugs his sleeve imploringly.*)

TOKIWAZU FULL CHORUS. (NAGAUTA *drums join the* SAMISEN *accompaniment.*)
I must! Alas, I must!
  A fiendish monster
  Waits at home!
LORD UKYO. (*He sinks to the floor in a dejected heap.*)
How annoying! Damn, damn, damn! (*In a fit of pique he kicks his heels against the floor.*)

NAGAUTA CHORUS LEADER.
In actual fact,
  He loves his wife.
He longs to see
  Her dear face so!
LORD UKYO. (*FADE MUSIC NO. 9. He sits up with a
start, and looks out at the audience incredulously.*)
What's that? Want to see the face of that old hag?
Yaips, what a thought! (*The thought is indeed too much
for him, and he rocks back and forth holding his head
in both hands. Then he looks up with a bright gleam in
his eyes, points to the audience with his closed fan, and
addresses us formally.*) I'll tell you exactly what I think,
to the tune of an old folk song!
TOKIWAZU CHORUS LEADER. (*MUSIC CUE NO. 10.
The lead* SAMISEN *strikes a resounding arpeggio. The*
CHORUS LEADER *then begins an* A CAPPELLA *chant in a
high-pitched voice.*)
Such a very
Strange face!
TOKIWAZU FULL CHORUS. (*The* TOKIWAZU SAMISEN
are joined by the NAGAUTA *flute and drums, and by the
off-stage right bass drum and bells as well. They strike
up a rollicking country melody. The bouncy rhythm soon
has* LORD UKYO *on his feet, miming the words of the*
CHORUS.*)
A bashed-in nose!
  And banjo eyes!
A black-as-pitch
  Complexion!
(LORD UKYO *scuttles over beside the robed figure, and
He makes circles with thumb and forefinger, and looks
out at us through them.*)
Why she looks for all the world like:
  A broken down
  Mangy
  Old monkey!
(LORD UKYO *scuttles over beside the robed figure, and*

poses in a MIE: *his face purposely hideous, his fingers extended like claws over* LADY TAMANOI'S *head. On the verge of discarding the robe, she stamps her foot repeatedly and bounces about on the cask.*)
Yes! Yes!
A decrepit old monkey who scratches around
  In the forest all day,
All drenched by the drizzling rain!

(*FADE MUSIC NO. 10.* LADY TAMANOI *explodes from the cask, knocking him far over to stage right. But he is so caught up in his act that he scarcely notices, and after circling the stage once in a loping, monkey-like gait, he collapses to the floor exhausted. Bit by bit her rage subsides. Finally he turns to her and speaks, a picture of jovial intoxication.*)

LORD UKYO. I think that's enough for a first installment, don't you Taro? Remember now, not one word of this to the old lady or you don't hear the rest of the story. Right? (*The robe trembles, then nods.*) Right! You can take off the robe now, Taro. (*He crosses to her and is about to snatch the robe, but she pulls away.*) You don't want to? You can't go on wearing it forever, you know, just because *you* feel like it. (*Her response is to huddle down even further inside the robe and to pull it ever more tightly around her.*) What a fellow you are. Come on now, let's see your face! (*No response.*) Off with it! (*No response.*) No? Then I'll do it for you! (*He grabs the robe from the right side. They struggle briefly.*)
TOKIWAZU FULL CHORUS. (SAMISEN *accompaniment only.*)
The robe flies off.
  My God! Not Taro!
  Out pops the devil herself!

(*Two* STAGE ASSISTANTS *whisk off the robe. One of them swiftly moves the cask out of the way as* LADY

TAMANOI *leaps to her feet. There is dead silence.*
LORD UKYO *freezes first in fear. Then he turns and
tries to steal silently away from the dread sight. One,
two, three, four steps. Then the dam bursts and*
LADY TAMANOI *lets loose a flood of abuse.* LORD
UKYO *drops to his knees as if shot. He doesn't dare
face her.*)

LADY TAMANOI. You villain! You villain! Try to fool
me and run off will you! Where did you go?
LORD UKYO. I . . . I . . . I . . . I . . . (*He bounces
up and down on his knees like a puppet on a string, his
hands waving helplessly in the air.*)
LADY TAMANOI. Where did you go? *Where did you go?*
LORD UKYO. To . . . to . . . to . . . to . . . the
. . . the . . . temple of the Five Hundred Buddhas!
LADY TAMANOI. In one night *to Kyushu? (She actually
growls.)* Liar, liar, liar! If you don't tell the truth, I'll
tear you to pieces! (*She crosses close behind him and
stamps savagely.) Tell me!*
LORD UKYO. Yes, yes, yes! (*On the verge of frantic
tears.*) I went to the . . . the . . . the . . . Z . . .
Z . . . Zen . . . Zenko Temple in . . . .
LADY TAMANOI. It's all lies! Lies! Ohh! Catch him
somebody! *Somebody catch him! (She beats her breast
and stamps thunderously on the floor.)*
LORD UKYO. (*He feels his end is near. Desperately he
tries to rise to his feet and flee. But his legs are paralyzed
by fear. Frantically he clasps his hands before him and
prays for all he is worth.*) Lord Buddha, save me, save
me, save me! Save me, Lord Buddha, save me!

(*MUSIC CUE NO. 11. In a flash* LADY TAMANOI *is on
him. She seizes his ear, throws him to the ground,
and beats him soundly. The audible sound of blows
mingles with his prayers and her continued torrent
of abuse. The theatrical quality of Kabuki is clearly
seen here, where the most violent action is converted*

*into stylized dance movement and performed in
strict time to the singing and music of the orchestra.*)

FULL CHORUS. (*With four* SAMISENS.)
Forgive me,
  Forgive me,
  Forgive me!
Wild excuses
  Pour from
  His lips!
A cascade
  Of rambling
  Gibberish!
(LORD UKYO *makes no attempt to resist and at length she
falls back out of sheer exhaustion.* LORD UKYO *sees this
as his opportunity to escape, and seizing the robe for
protection, he stumbles to his feet. But he isn't fast
enough. She grabs the trailing end of the robe and stops
him short. First he pulls, then she pulls, in rhythmic
movement, as they struggle for possession of the robe.
They both jerk hard at the same time and the robe flies
from their hands. They fall to the floor, momentarily
stunned, he stage left and she stage right. A* STAGE
ASSISTANT *scurries forward and spreads the robe out full
next to where* LORD UKYO *lies sprawled on his back.*)
Lying
  Deceitful
  Philanderer!
I won't forgive!
  I won't!
  I won't!
She thunders furiously!
Hard on his heels
  She chases!
In panic
  He flees
  He flees!

.

(From here on the remainder of the play is executed as pure dance-pantomime. All the on-stage musicians, playing together for the first time, take up a highly rhythmic folk melody, its metronome-like quality accented by the addition of the booming off-stage right drums. Still sprawled on the floor, when his head pops up, hers bobs down; when his bobs down, hers pops up. One, two, three times. Jerking in exact time to the music, on every fourth strong beat, they seem like marionettes with all the strings cut but one. Now they begin to move their arms and legs as well, in angular, jerky movements. The effect is like seeing a series of stopped motion pictures. He tries to escape her by burrowing under the spread-out robe; he is a great, gold caterpillar worming his way across the stage. Simultaneously, she heaves and drags herself along the floor supported on one arm, the other groping the air wildly for him. As he inches right, she flounders left, until they cross paths and stop dead center stage. They are inches apart, back to back, unaware of each other's presence. She pauses to catch her breath, she looks frantically about—has he escaped? He pokes his head gingerly out from under the robe—has she gone? The robe slips to his shoulders, and with a broad smile of relief, he sits up. The music tapers off. Silence. Then in unison they look back over their shoulders. They see each other at the same time and fall back in surprise. The music begins again with a crash of drums, and takes up the same melody as before. Once more LORD UKYO staggers to his feet and tries to move away, but his legs still fail to function and all he can do is to flail about. The robe starts to fall off; his hair is in wild disarray; his face is quivering in terror. LADY TAMANOI rises to her knees, then to her feet, still violently shaking with rage. Her arms are outstretched, her fingers curled into claws that grasp futilely for his tender flesh. By degrees, he begins

to inch his way stage right and step by step she follows. In rhythm to the music, they move in unison, gesticulating grotesquely: she chases, he flees. They are still working their way across the stage when the light silk Kabuki curtain, of traditional rust, green and black stripes is run swiftly before them by a black-hooded STAGE ATTENDANT [KUROGO]. *For a moment the music continues, then stops. FADE MUSIC NO. 11. The play is over.*)

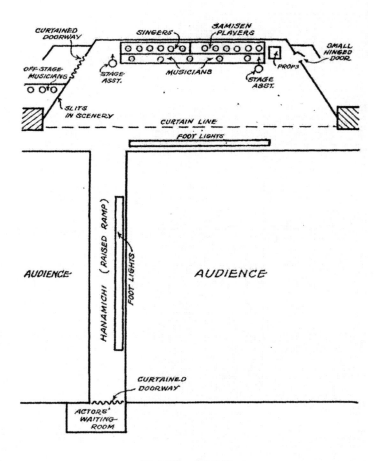

FLOOR PLAN
"KANJINCHO"

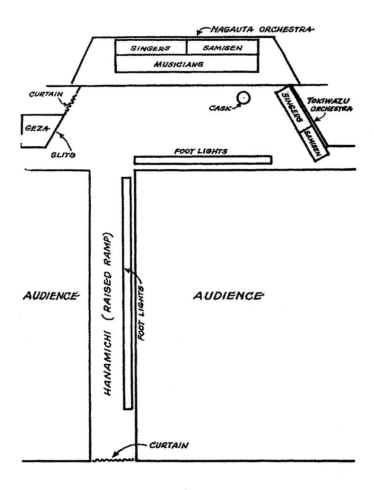

FLOOR PLAN
"THE ZEN SUBSTITUTE"

A

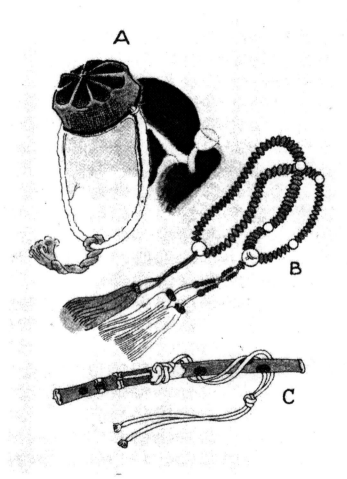

B

C

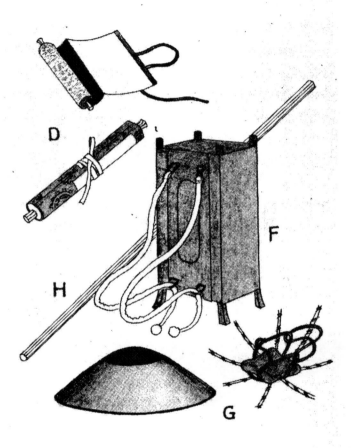

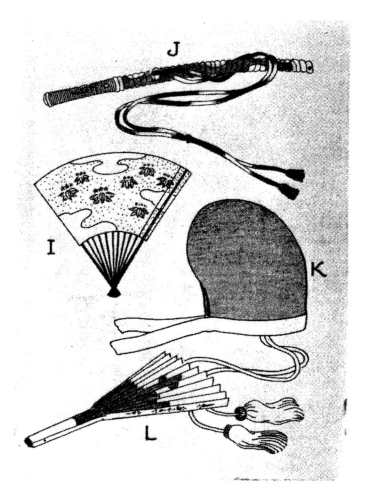

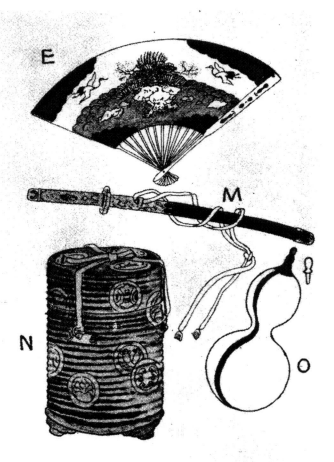

P

Q

OTHER TITLES AVAILABLE FROM SAMUEL FRENCH

TREASURE ISLAND
Ken Ludwig

All Groups / Adventure / 10m, 1f (doubling) / Areas
Based on the masterful adventure novel by Robert Louis
Stevenson, *Treasure Island* is a stunning yarn of piracy on
the tropical seas. It begins at an inn on the Devon coast
of England in 1775 and quickly becomes an unforget-
table tale of treachery and mayhem featuring a host of
legendary swashbucklers including the dangerous Billy
Bones (played unforgettably in the movies by Lionel Bar-
rymore), the sinister two-timing Israel Hands, the brassy
woman pirate Anne Bonney, and the hideous form of
evil incarnate, Blind Pew. At the center of it all are Jim
Hawkins, a 14-year-old boy who longs for adventure, and
the infamous Long John Silver, who is a complex study
of good and evil, perhaps the most famous hero-villain of
all time. Silver is an unscrupulous buccaneer-rogue whose
greedy quest for gold, coupled with his affection for Jim,
cannot help but win the heart of every soul who has ever
longed for romance, treasure and adventure.

OTHER TITLES AVAILABLE FROM SAMUEL FRENCH

MURDER AT CAFÉ NOIR
David Landau
Music and Lyrics by Nikki Stern

Mystery / 4m, 3f / Interior

The most popular mystery dinner show in the country, *Murder at Café Noir* has enjoyed weekly productions coast to coast since its premiere in 1989. This forties detective story come to life features Rick Archer, P.I., out to find a curvaceous runaway on the forgotten island of Mustique, a place stuck in a black and white era. The owner of the Café Noir has washed ashore, murdered, and Rick's quarry was the last person seen with him. He employs his hard boiled talents to find the killer. Was it the French madame and club manager, the voodoo priestess, the shyster British attorney, the black marketeer or the femme fatale? The audience votes twice on what they want Rick to do next and these decisions change the flow of this comic tribute to the Bogart era.

"Fast and funny satire."
– *Los Angeles Times*

This whodunit is darn good it's the kind of show that lingers on you mind, like a dame's perfume
– *Maryland Journal*